The Consumption of Kuala Lumpur

TOPOGRAPHICS

The Consumption of Kuala Lumpur

Ziauddin Sardar

REAKTION BOOKS

For Zain, who shared my journeys

Published by Reaktion Books Ltd
79 Farringdon Road, London EC1M 3JU
www.reaktionbooks.co.uk

First published 2000

Colour printed by BAS Printers Ltd, Over Wallop, Hampshire
Printed and bound in Great Britain by Biddles Ltd, Guildford
and King's Lynn

British Library Cataloguing in Publication Data

Sardar, Ziauddin
    The consumption of Kuala Lumpur. – (Topographics)
    1. Kuala Lumpur (Malaysia) – Civilization
    I. Title
    959.5'154

ISBN 1 86189 057 5

Contents

Provinces (faint, top left)

Meklong · Bangpason

Tavoy I. · Mergui · Chantibon

Kings I. · Tungyai

Terasserim · Penor

Domel I. · Gulf of Siam

Sullivan I. · Koh-dud

St. Mathews I. · Carnom · Pan-jang

Chaiya · Pt. Camb

Tueop · Larchin Id.

Seiyer · Ligor

Ponga · Penjay · Tantalam

Strait

Selang or Junkseylon · Madalung or Talung · C. Patani

Payang · Lantao · Patani

Way I. · Salang or Junkseylon · Queda · Redang

Lanta · Portis

Tellibon · Tredi

Lancarol · Wellesley Province · Tringanon

Samalanga · Penang or Pr. of Wales · Tingoran · Kapas

Passier

Acheen · Perak

Analaboo · Delhi · Pahang

Likar · Salangore · Mt. Ophir

Batubarra · Mukot

Tabi or Hog I. · Tarumon · Lidang · Malacca

Baniak I. · Asahan · Tobah · Johore

Nias · Tapanooly · Bangkaho · Siak

Tapanooly · Batam

Natal · Siak

Pilots I. · Ayer · tingies · Indragirie

Passamo · Tiko · Sankara R.

Mintao or Batu · Ophir

Equator

The View from Menarah Indahh

I

The apartment building stands perched on the lip of a great earthen bowl. Behind and above are high ridges formed by folds of thick jungle, rather like the prinked edges of a piecrust. Below the lip, the ground falls away in a wide swathe where houses nestle among trees and, far away on the western horizon, the skyscrapers of the city stand out like tall trees breaking the line of the canopy forest. The little balcony of my living room takes in the whole, grand sweep. Laid out for closest inspection, just outside the precincts of the apartment building, is the full synthetic glory and lush nitrated greenery of Kelab Darul Ehsan, a golf and recreation club for folks in newly acquired circumstances. Around the Kelab winds a circular footpath, the local joggers' highway, always jog-jammed between 5 a.m. and 9 a.m., and again in the evening peak hours until the leisurely after-dinner strollers emerge. In between, the footpath is left to bake gently in the sun or become the bed of a torrential river in the rain. When I walk this footpath, conformity having its effect, I look through the gaps between trees, shrubs and houses back to the condominium and I see the building lost in the jungle from every vantage point. From around the lip, from down in the dip, whichever way you approach or look, there, in its mouldering isolation, is the last lonely condo before the jungle. This is Menarah Indahh, the block of flats where I have been living for the past few years. Menarah Indahh is in Taman TAR; the TAR is an acronym – most things go by an acronym in Kuala Lumpur. The TAR stands for Tun Abdul Razak, a former prime minister. The neighbourhood, Taman TAR (Garden Tun Abdul Razak), is a developers' vision of gracious modern living that has colonized the head of a little valley leading back up into the

Detail of a 17th-century Dutch map of the Malay archipelago.   7

Present-day peninsular Malaysia.

jungle. Taman TAR itself is part of Ampang Jaya, and Ampang Jaya is both in the state of Selangor and a suburb of Kuala Lumpur, or KL as everyone refers to it. The road gently meanders down the hill in wide sweeps until it meets the larger road, Jalan Ulu Klang, which takes you in one direction to the Zoo, and in the other to the major thoroughfare of Jalan Ampang. Jalan Ampang houses most of the foreign embassies and this international enclave leads on into the city.

I watch the sunset. It does not take much time: one moment the sun is there, and it is day, and the next it has disappeared. The floodlights of Kelab Darul Ehsan come on immediately, synchronized with the sunset. The Asian work ethic predominates here, meaning long hours at the office and a five-and-half-day working week. So time for play, a distinct legacy of colonial times, like the rest of the upwardly mobile lifestyle, must be accommodated after working hours: hence, floodlit golf. Air around me condenses. It becomes a gentle blanket that does not quite constitute rain; it does not really come down but materializes in the atmosphere. I notice some clouds moving swiftly over the horizon; they come and hover in front of the building, as though thinking, and then quietly drift into my living room. For a moment I think it might rain inside my apartment. But the clouds simply nestle around me and everything becomes soggy. A pair of large butterflies drift inside and settle on the wall near the curtains.

I know them well. Huge and stunningly beautiful, they are utterly devoted to each other. Predominantly black with a row of green triangles on their wings, which have a span of about fifteen centimetres, they carry a bright red band around their heads. Their technical appellation, *Trogonoptera brookiana*, deprives them of their sublime charm. I have named them after the lovers in the classical Persian romance, *Laila Majnun*. They were said to be 'black' and so in love that they became oblivious to the dangers of earthly existence. Laila, consumed by her love for Majnun, dies; and Majnun, unable to live without Laila, commits suicide. I do not wish these winged lovers to have a similar end; but there is a constant danger lurking on the walls and ceiling of my flat. And the feeling that a tragedy of Persian proportions is about to unfold in my presence overwhelms me. First thing every morning, I rush to the living room and breathe a sigh of relief when I find them waiting for me to open the balcony doors and release them to the jungle.

The threat comes from three generations of geckoes dwelling behind various picture frames that decorate the walls. I have watched them grow and multiply, play and fight. I have developed a relationship with the patriarch. Indeed, I have even managed to train him: on my instruction 'Go fetch, Grandpa!', he moves like lightning to gobble up troublesome visitors. Life in a tropical climate requires the balcony doors to remain open all waking hours to facilitate the circulation of air. This provides plenty of opportunity for a plethora of troublesome visitors to make their appearance: mosquitoes (including giant ones carrying the deadly dengue), giant wasps, giant three-horn rhino beetles, longhorned grasshoppers, cockroaches and many unknown, curious varieties. There is, for example, a form of winged frog – not a frog, in fact, but a beetle resembling nothing so much as a frog, right down to its beige and brown markings. Its body is so solid and heavy it seems impossible for its transparent, gossamer wings to have the strength to propel it anywhere, and yet it regularly flies in through the balcony and goes slamming with loud thuds into the walls of the living room. Plenty of opportunity too for the welcome visitors: the hosts of little butterflies, so beautifully marked they take your breath away. The colours and patterns of many of them resemble the finest Indonesian batik, and I cannot help wondering if the delicate tracery of the human art is not, after all, a mere pale imitation of the naturally occurring form. Some days the ceiling of the living room is a carpet of butterflies, dicing with extinction as the family of juniors, the geckoes, contemplate a feast. The problem is that the younger members of the family do not listen to me. They run around the walls and ceiling assaulting everything they come across, even though they can't always swallow what they attack. I fear, one day, they will disturb the tranquillity of Laila Majnun; or worse kill one of them, which would mean self-immolation for the other.

At about the same time that Laila Majnun come in, a flock of bats flurry into motion. During the day, these bats are invisible – they are obviously there somewhere, hanging upside down, sleeping, contemplating, dreaming. But as soon as the sun sinks, large swarms of them swirl, swing, form infinite loops, moving with great speed in what appear to be chaotic movements. Occasionally, a bat flies into the living room, its high-velocity entrance generating the fear that it will hit the wall and splatter itself all over the floor. But, in fact, they keep swirling around, like demented, would-be kamikazes with me as the cowering aircraft carrier. Once inside, its zooming fly-past describes ever-wider circles, with sudden tangential dives in another direction in search of an exit. A strange dance follows: I sheepishly skirt the kamikaze, negotiating my way towards all the doors and windows, open them, then carefully work my way back to a convenient point and try to 'shoo' it out. It takes a considerable time for this eccentric minuet with a kamikaze to result in the bat identifying an opening and then exiting stage left. Invariably, the bats enter by way of the balcony and make egress through the front door, which is at the back of the building facing the jungle.

The door opens straight on to the forest. Even though it is inside a metropolitan jungle, the Ampang forest is a real rainforest, no holds barred. The term jungle is really applicable only to secondary forests where growth is relentless, unbridled, apparently quite beyond the control of Man. Here, the rays of the sun have direct access to the forest floor fostering a growth that is denied to other forests in which the canopy is too dense. Several massive *tualang* trees, over sixty metres high, stand majestically only a few metres away from the door. They are described as 'emergent' trees and produce commercially valuable timber. Below these large trees is the dense layer of the canopy, under which there is another layer of trees, about ten metres high, consisting of saplings. The forest floor is covered with thick layers of shrubs; in undisturbed rainforests, this layer is fairly open and easy to travel through. But in Ampang's secondary forest, or *belukar*, the vegetation is almost impenetrable. There are many strange plants here, such as the blue-leaved *Selaginella*, which have adapted to growing in dark places. Different layers of plants provide different habitats for the animals. Hornbills, gibbons, the slow loris and many insects live in the upper canopy. Pheasants, porcupines, pig-tailed monkeys and insects live on the forest floor. Males of the Rajah Brooke Birdwing butterfly fly near the ground, particularly near the open areas of

11

running water. I just open my front door and get a sideways on, complete floor-to-ceiling view of it all. The forest is never silent, but it does function as a very precise alarm clock. Just before the morning *azan*, the call to prayer from the local mosque, the forest wakes up and every living thing it contains leaves off its nightly noises for a full-throated, various, discrete burst of sound that rises to a crescendo. When everyone has announced their presence and asked what's for breakfast, they subside into the normal day-long throb of background sound. The open space, a few metres wide, between the forest and Menarah Indahh, is occupied by a silted riverbed. Most of the time there is just a pleasant sound of trickling water that descends from a ledge opposite the fifth floor, my floor, and drips down to become a narrow rivulet that winds across the silted bed, before ducking into a culvert. When it rains the scene is transformed. They say Kuala Lumpur means muddy junction, but I swear it's onomatopoeic, signifying the junction where lumps-pour, where it pours down lumps of rain. The first time I was caught walking in the rain it physically hurt; I was enveloped in a solid wall of stinging, pounding, pricking needles of rain with no way out. When the rain comes, the trickle of water becomes a torrent, a thundering debouchement of orange-brown water carrying laterite soil in suspension that overleaps the ledge, plunging with deafening roar to the ground beneath. The quiet silted bed becomes a raging river, set fair for, but never quite, washing away the building. It can rain at any time throughout the year in Malaysia; during the two monsoon seasons it rains even more. The monsoons are notable for the great thunderstorms with their spectacular *son et lumière* displays that literally turn day into night. Butterflies and bats are not the only things that come in via my balcony: one day a bolt of lightning attempted to play the same game.

The trees forming the forest wall behind the building were not only home to the waterfall; they also housed a troupe of monkeys. These were the long-tailed macaques which the Malays call *kera*, after its call, according to their onomatopoeic method for naming much of their fauna. These monkeys have pouches in their cheeks, to store their food before eating. They are very greedy: always stuffing their pouches with food, and constantly looking for more. They move in the forest as a family unit, swinging from branch to branch with their long and powerful arms, whooping and screaming with abandon. Amongst its own kind, this troupe is extremely gentle and very well behaved: the babies clinging to their mother's bellies, the adults swinging from branch to branch, picking fruits, opening them with their teeth, eating some, dropping some, giving to the young, chatting and picking lice from each other. But as soon as they see a human they transmute into another kind of creature. First they shriek and jump up and down as though in a state of panic. Then, they herd together and become aggressive. If the human gets too close, they attack in unison. Menarah Indahh, being a fully functional condo, has its own swimming pool, set across the road from the main building in a steep, tropical dinglely dell, that falls away under the lip on which the building and road stand. You get to this secluded place through a tunnel that underpasses the road and down exercise-inducing flights of stairs. The monkeys like to pay visits to the swimming pool. They troop over the road and then rappel down the tree-clad slopes and clamber all over the clubhouse that houses squash courts and saunas. Once my infant son was taking an explorative ramble around the various floors of the clubhouse while the rest of our party lazed by the pool. Interested, as any youngster is, in wildlife, he got too close to the monkeys who were at that very time also clambering about the clubhouse. So a large male with vicious teeth leapt to the attack. Naturally enough, my son leapt in the opposite direction and tried to run away, along the perplexing network of stairways that weave their way around the building, pursued by the gathering troupe. Once we were alerted by his cries for help, it took some effort to effect a rescue. A disorganized massed phalanx of panicked, squash racket-wielding adults made a desperate, uncoordinated dash for the sound of his voice. Eventually, after many wrong turns, and futile yells of moral support, we managed to place ourselves between him and the monkeys and impress upon them that *this* troupe was not to be trifled with.

A leisurely walk anywhere in the vicinity of Menarah Indahh was always full of surprises.

II

Menarah Indahh itself does not have a memory. It is just a rather ugly block of flats perched half-way up a mountain: a lame offering to modernity. It is new, no more than five years old, though already ageing fast; as interlopers in the jungle do, it has acquired a patina of mould and is beset by ants and living things of all description, shape, hue and kind. But the forest is full of memories. It talks of the monsoon winds, the Indian Ocean world, the nearby port of Malacca, of civilizations that have left an unerasable mark on this land.

The *tualang* trees are old enough to remember the story of Rajah Iskander Shah, a descendant of Alexander the Great, who long ago became the ruler of Tumasek, on the island of Singapore. Now, Iskander had a weak spot for women and, despite already having several wives, he forced the beautiful daughter of his grand vizier to join his harem. The other wives became very jealous; they succeeded in alienating the rajah from his young wife. So Iskander had the poor woman impaled in the bazaar. The grand vizier promised revenge and invited the powerful Javanese King of Majapahit to come and conquer Tumasek. The King of Majapahit sent a massive fleet. As the battle began, Iskander asked the grand vizier to provide rice for his soldiers. The grand vizier told the rajah that all the rice in Singapore had run out. At dawn, he opened the gates and allowed the Javanese to enter the city. The Javanese brutally massacred the inhabitants of the city. Divine retribution was visited on the grand vizier for his treachery. His rice turned into dirt; he and his wife were turned into stone.

Iskander escaped to the mainland where he was attacked by a herd of large iguanas. His soldiers had to kill many giant lizards to save themselves – so many in fact that the carcasses of the lizards became a mountain and gave off an obnoxious smell. That place is still there and is called Biawak Busok, the stinking iguana. Iskander continued to flee and arrived at a coastal area. While resting under the shade of a tree, his dog was attacked by a *kanchil*, the small mouse-deer. The tiny deer kicked so hard that the poor dog fell into the water. Iskander was so impressed by the strength and courage of the miniature deer that he decided to build a city at that spot. As he was resting under a malacca tree, he called the place Malacca.

So begins *Sejarah Malayu*, the ancient chronicles of the Malays. To understand Kuala Lumpur, one has to understand *Sejarah Malayu*, a riproaring narrative, full of adventure, history, myth, migration, poetry and wordplay, where people experience migration, uprooting, disjuncture and metamorphosis. It is both fiction and history; and, as befits such a postmodern epic, it has no dates. Some scholars date it from the Portuguese period, while others claim it was commissioned by Sultan Abdullah of Malacca who reigned from 1610 to 1621. According to *Sejarah Malayu*, Islam came to Malaya as a result of a dream: in a dream Rajah Kechil Besar, a descendant of Iskander, saw the Prophet Muhammad who told him that a ship would arrive from Jeddah and he should follow what the crew told him. Sure enough a ship arrived and its crew converted the rajah and his subjects to Islam. The rajah changed his name to Sultan Muhammad Shah. Modernist scholars, more concerned with dates and the exact nature of historical events, have suggested that Islam first arrived in the Malay peninsula in the fourteenth century. The argument centred on the oldest-known Malay text: an inscription found on a broken granite tombstone in Trengganu, on the east coast of the peninsula. In the 1920s, C. O. Blagdon, an English Orientalist, provided 21 theoretical possible alternative dates for the inscription, but settled for 788 Hejrah (1386 CE) as the most probable. There the matter rested until, in 1970, through an ingenious variety of logical, mathematical, linguistic, cultural, philosophical and mystical arguments, the Malay scholar, Muhammad Naguib al-Attas, proved *The Correct Date of the Trengganu Inscription: Friday, 4th Rajab, 702 AH/Friday, 22nd February, 1303* AC. It is therefore reasonable to assume that Islam first appeared in Malaysia in the late thirteenth century; and the inscription probably commemorates a crewmember of the ship from Jeddah.

Of course, the history of Malaya did not begin with the coming of Islam. These primeval forests have primeval memories that stretch back to the dawn of Malay civilization and the various cycles of incorporation that mark its progress. But Malaysian history has become a kind of forgetting, a specially constructed framework of discrete, disconnected boxes, each of which suggests commencement from a certain point before which there was only emptiness and silence. But the forest is never silent. You have to get beyond this kind of history to uncover the vibrant story of enterprise witnessed and remembered by the forests. Compartmentalized history is a special artefact of Western learning, for specialized purposes, assiduously assimilated by peoples all round the globe. The *Sejarah Malayu* is nothing like that. It assumes and absorbs and refers to history while remaining preoccupied with its own concerns. For nearly seven hundred years Malays have cherished the understanding that to be a Malay is to be a Muslim. In that understanding there is a whole world of meaning, being and knowing; it does not eradicate but absorbs into itself all that was, is and will be.

So what was? Malaysia was, according to a gentleman called John Milton, the Golden Chersonese, the golden peninsula. The source of his epithet was ancient but the notice he took of it was filled with contemporary relevance for a man of affairs in London of the mid-1600s. In Book XI of *Paradise Lost*, Milton has Adam taken up on to a promontory by the Archangel Michael 'To show him all earth's kingdoms and their glory . . . City of old or modern fame'. The panoramic sweep jumps around a bit, but it takes in China and India: 'To Agra and Lahor of great Mogul, Down to the golden Chersonese'. It includes Persia, Muscovy, Byzantium, Ethiopia, around the coast of Africa, from Mombasa to Angola and Congo, the Niger bend to Morocco and Algiers until he gets across the Mediterranean to Rome, then on to take in the Mexico of Montezuma and the Peru of Atahualpa. This was essentially the entire newly discovered world of vital interest to the enterprise of Empire that was just getting underway in England. And there, in pride of place, amongst all the glories Adam saw, was Malaysia. Why? The answer, like Milton's knowledge, is both ancient and modern.

It was Pomponious Mela in AD 43 who made the first reference to something that can be identified as Malaysia in European writing. He spoke of Chryse, a peninsula where the soil was of gold, and Argyre, an island off the coast of this peninsula where the soil was of silver. Chryse is identified as Malaysia because at this time alluvial gold was collected and traded from there. The snippet of fantasized information was acquired through Rome's increasing interest in the acquisition of luxury

The Trengganu inscription (above, detail) and a typical Malay tombstone from Sebarag Tok Soh, Sungai Petani, believed to be 300 years old.

17

goods. This upwardly mobile consumerism caused them to take, or allow their Greek employees to take, more particular notice of the information available in the Levant and Western Asia about the lands beyond India. Despite Alexander the Great's foray to the fringes of 'Al Hind', the great names of classical Greek writing had little direct information on the East. The real giveaway is that a solid vision of a world beyond the limited circuit of Europe arises only from reading the *Periplus of the Erythraean Sea*, as the Indian Ocean was called. The author of this first-century AD piece of essential reading declares his work to be 'written by a merchant for the use of merchants'. And the author was not European at all, but a Graeco-Egyptian. In contrast to the fabulous tales that dominate the writings of Greece and Rome, the birthplace of inventing Other peoples, the Egyptian merchant presents a non-literary compendium on the trade routes and ports of call of the Indian Ocean. The merchant's regular stamping ground went no further than the Malabar coast of India, but he passes on information of the onward connections as far as China, that is, beyond Malaysia and the Spice Islands of Indonesia. This prosaic work offers a glimpse of a complete world, one into which Europe is barely intruding. The creation of this world beyond the bounds of Europe had a great deal to do with the enterprise and creativity of the peoples of the Malay archipelago – and that's what really made this Chersonese golden.

Conventional history still has only an indistinct grasp of what actually happened in this part of the world. Most historians agree that from earliest times the Malay peninsula has been a thoroughfare for the dispersal of peoples originating on the Asian continent. The forests were alive with movement of peoples who went on to inhabit the Southeast Asian archipelago, that is, the thousands of islands that comprise the modern states of Indonesia and the Philippines, and on to the Micronesian, Melanesian and Polynesian islands of the Pacific. Every rock overhang in the interior of the peninsula has evidence of early residence by neolithic peoples. The jump is from shreds and patches of the vaguest early prehistory to the period from 500 BC to AD 500 when recorded things begin to happen. About 500 BC is when classical Greek civilization swung into action. Greece had precious little knowledge of the world east of their 'barbarian' nemesis, Persia. You get a good insight into this relationship in Gore Vidal's novel *Creation*. With his usual asperity Vidal reminds us that while Greece was emerging Babylon, one seat of the Persian Empire, looked back on 2,000 years of continuous history. He also makes the point that the classical age of ancient Greece was contemporaneous with the age of the Buddha in India and Zoroaster in Persia. In particular, I relish his elegant put-downs of the *nouveau arriviste* Greeks, the point being that where Greek literature keeps on spinning out fabulous tales of golden anthills and monstrous peoples, out east, in the vague lands beyond Persia, obviously something was happening to arouse the money-minded interest of these pompous, opinionated Greeks.

Roman learning was acquired from the Greeks, not least in the sense that writers, tutors and travellers who worked for the Roman Empire were usually Greek slaves. So we arrive back at the era of Pomponious Mela and the first mention of Malaysia. As Rome secured its grip on the Middle Eastern provinces of its empire a new luminary adds to the store of reference to Malaysia. This is Claudius Ptolemy, who also refers to the Golden Chersonese. Ptolemy is a rather shadowy figure, who hailed from Egypt and was active in the middle of the second century AD. His *Geographica*, a standard work of the ancient and early modern world, is notable for its long-delayed seminal legacy. His considerable underestimation of the size of the earth caused a certain Christopher Columbus to set sail to the west with the intention of arriving in the fabled, golden lands of the east. Another good reason for Columbus to go east via the west is that Ptolemy believed the Indian Ocean was an enclosed sea, there being a landmass, Terra Incognita Australis, linking the end of Africa to the Malay peninsula. So there was no way to China following the Portuguese prescription of sailing along the coast of Africa.

Anyway, we know trade reached Rome from China, both via the millennia-old land routes and thanks to sea-borne trade across the Indian Ocean. Hence conventional history tends to credit Rome, and especially its Greek employees, with being the key ingredient in unlocking of the secret of the monsoon winds. This piece of oft-repeated 'wisdom' is basically akin to the generally accepted notion that in 1498 Vasco da Gama, following in the long-pursued Portuguese strategy, down and around Africa, 'discovered' India. Da Gama rounded the southern tip of Africa, as Bartolemeo Dias had done before him, and sailed north until he hit the bustling port of Malindi where he hired a Muslim pilot, fully conversant with the busy sea routes, who led his little convoy to Calicut in India. The apocryphal tale is that this pilot was ibn Majid, the author of at least fourteen books on geography and related matters. Da Gama's latest biographer, my friend Sanjay Subramarniam, disputes that the pilot was in fact ibn Majid, though he asserts it most definitely was a local Muslim pilot, and like me enjoys the implicit put-down of the apocryphal identification. The historian John Hale notes that when da Gama landed at Calicut he was met by two Tunisian merchants who inquired, in Spanish, why he had bothered to make the journey, the trade routes to India being no mystery, except to Europeans. In other words, the knowledge of the Indian Ocean world belonged to the peoples of that world. Just as da Gama benefited from it, so it is likely that the Romans benefited from local knowledge. It is merely European hubris, and the need to stress supposed European superiority in the age of Empire – ancient, modern and postmodern – that requires the Romans and Greeks to be inventors of all knowledge. So tangential was the Far East to the bread and circuses and let's-get-on-with-the-blood-and-licentiousness mentality of Rome, and so far were they from being inquisitive explorers, that the thesis of conventional history is best considered, as Henry Ford put it, as bunk. Once conventional history has allowed the Romans to discover the essential mechanism that makes the Indian Ocean world work, it immediately forgets about the

20

region, it being of no further interest or importance until da Gama hoves into view to make his earth-shattering 'discovery'. Had it not been for the continuing history of the world made by the peoples of this 'forgotten backwater', of course, there would have been no impetus for European powers to spend a century earnestly trying to arrive in India and the Spice Islands of the East Indies. But somehow this is the logical unconnective tissue by which conventional history operates.

The monsoon winds by which the Indian Ocean world operates are two cycles of regular wind changes, from southwest to northeast. The winds allow sailing ships to go from East Africa to Southeast Asia and then return on the reverse winds that also enable ships from China to sail as far as India. The regularity and convenience of these winds makes Southeast Asia the hub around which the Indian Ocean world swirls. Sometime in the first century AD this became known, marginally, in Europe. Exactly when and how it became known in and around the Indian Ocean is not recorded. What is evident is that in the early centuries AD trade within and around the Indian Ocean gathers pace. It becomes possible to identify new centres of trade that arise, have their day and then fade from view. It is rather like watching a firefly display in the mangrove swamps that cluster around the coasts and estuaries. It is within these cycles of episodic history that Malaysia belongs.

The successive centres of civilization founded on trade become apparent, within their own compartments of history, with the publication in 1904 of G. Coedes's *The Indianized States of Southeast Asia*. Coedes's work remains the standard text on this subject; and anyone who attempts to understand Kuala Lumpur and this region must travel via Coedes. What he reveals is the close inter-relationship between India and Southeast Asia, partners in creating this dynamic system. The other pole that has exerted an important influence on Southeast Asia is China. Chinese expansionism was one factor that caused many peoples from what is now southern China to move into Indo-China and down the Malay peninsula. Indian influence

21

was more pervasive. In Southeast Asia it led to the creation of distinctive regional variation on common cultural threads. Indianized languages, scripts, texts, practices are also identifiably and distinctively Thai, Khmer, Burmese and Javanese, among a whole host of others. The two greatest monuments in Indonesia are testimonies to this new era: Prambenam and Borobodur. The legacy of these centres survives and is evident because they are edifices in stone. Prambenam is a major Hindu temple complex near Yogjakarta in central Java. Borobodur, the largest Buddhist temple complex in the world, is also on Java. You can take a day trip from Yogjakarta and visit both sites. In Hindu tradition dancing was a sacred art, learned in the temple, where religious text found re-enactment as performance. So you can watch Katakali dancing in South India, or Thai classical dance, or watch the Ramayana dance groups in Indonesia to witness the legacy of the Indianized Ocean world. The basis of these traditions is the same epic, the Ramayana, yet it is not one but many texts in India and throughout Southeast Asia. Similarly, each dance style is noticeably different, as is the music that accompanies it. There is a Malayan Ramayana, on which the traditional performance of *wayang kulit*, the shadow puppet play, is based. In each place these cultural influences took on a life of their own, developed their own discrete style, began their own trajectories of civilizational flowering, while testifying to living, ongoing interconnections. The Kerala and Malabar coasts of South India not only share a cultural tradition with Southeast Asia; they look and feel amazingly like Malaysia as a physical environment, and have undergone exactly the same colonizing remake from the Portuguese, the Dutch and the British.

The beginnings of contact between India and Southeast Asia probably date back beyond the era of the birth of Greek civilization. The first major centre of Indianized civilization was Funan, covering an area that straddles the present boundaries of Cambodia and southern Vietnam. Funan becomes an historic reality in the first century AD. The notable events were happening at the edge of the reach of Europe. The Indian Ocean world is a

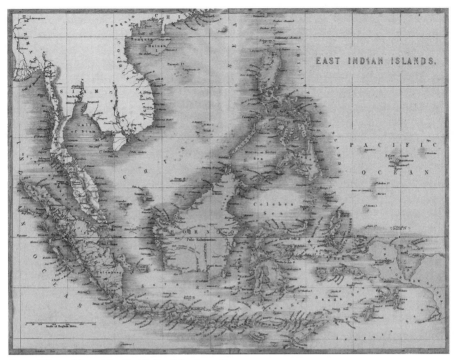

James Virtue, Map of the *East Indian Islands, c. 1850*.

world of maritime contact and many of the innovations in sea-faring technology that enabled the successive trading centres to establish wide spheres of influence were actually made in the most maritime of all areas in this world, the Malay archipelago. The Malay world is vast extent of coastal settlement on the peninsula and the thousands of islands. The Roman writer Pliny, who died in AD 79, makes a reference to trade across the Indian Ocean carried out on rafts, which would be a proximate description of Malay double outrigger canoes. These 'rafts' came bearing cinnamon, and the Greek word for this delicious spice derives from a Malayo-Polynesian word, through Phoenician and Hebrew, a sort of linguistic route map of the means by which the product, which originated in southern China, arrived in Europe. The most characteristic vessel of the China Seas, commonly known to us as the junk, derives its name from a Malay word *jang*. According to the experts, it was most likely developed by the Malays and acquired by other peoples in the extensive trading world that stretched from China to East Africa. By this time, the first century AD, Malay sailors had already reached Madagascar, the island off the east coast of southern Africa, carrying with them a number of native Southeast Asian plants including coconuts, bananas and cocoyam. Their descendants are still there and still speaking a Malayo-Polynesian language.

The history of the Indian Ocean world does not lend itself to easy manipulation for nationalistic purposes. Who exactly were the Malays who sailed to Madagascar? What was their starting point? We don't, and probably never will, know. The term Malay has a broad spectrum of meaning and contemporary Malaysians have an unfortunate tendency to assume that in such historical contexts it means only Indonesians. National history is very much a European creation and became a fad in the era of independence movements in the 'Third World'. The Middle Eastern scholar, George Hourani, goes to inordinate pains in his classic work, *Arab Seafaring*, merely to establish the point that important contributions were made to the technology of Indian Ocean seaborne trade by recognizably ethnic Arabs. Inspired by pan-Arab nationalism, the political context in which he wrote his book, he saw it as supremely important to disassemble the dominant thesis that Arabs were merely subordinate recipients of Greek and Roman achievement. In proving his point Hourani somehow fails to concentrate on the real importance of a world system beyond the reach of Europe that defied easy nationalism because it was cosmopolitan, interdependent and interactive.

The successive centres of civilization from Funan to Champa, a Malay coastal civilization in Vietnam, Pegu in Burma, Angkhor Wat in Cambodia, Sri Vijaya on Sumatra and Majapahit in northeast Java seldom confine themselves to proper nationalist pigeonholes. History in Southeast Asia marches to its own rhythms; the spheres of influence of all these great trading centres blithely overrun contemporary national borders. Trade was more than geographical connective tissue. Local trade fed into and merged with wider trading links and their political and social implications; along trade routes ideas, knowledge and cultural patterns found their own niches. This is true of the entire region from East Africa to China. It is known, for example, that Buddhism reached China across the Hindu Kush land route. It is also known that Buddhist pilgrims from China used the sea route via the Malay archipelago as a pathway to India, where the Hindu reform movement that became Buddhism was born. However, many Chinese pilgrims never went any further than Java, where they found extensive centres of Buddhist learning, in local language and script. The major centres were connected to smaller centres. Sri Vijaya held sway and received tribute from whole swathes of territory far removed from its location near the modern city of Palembang on southern Sumatra. Its tributary states spread over Java and the Malay peninsula. None of the succeeding empires in the region was confined to one island. At time of the founding of the Malacca sultanate, one finds that a certain Permeswara, possibly a descendant of the ruling dynasty of Sri Vijaya, goes by way of Java before arriving at Tumasek, or Singapore. Later he fetches up on the Malay peninsula in the modern state of Johoree before setting down roots at Malacca where he becomes known to the *Sejarah Malayu* as Rajah Iskander Shah. To establish the importance and legitimacy of his newly established centre of operations, Permeswara/Iskander sent an embassy to China. There is nothing of the backwater nor of the enclosed inward-looking little-state mentality at work in the history of the Indian Ocean world. This world emerged, developed, interacted and made itself rich, sophisticated, knowledgeable and skilled without reference to Europe. It did not exist only in the flickers of light conventional history can throw on a specific piece of earth. Its existence flourished in the ongoing operation of civilizational patterns that held prominence from certain promontories, while simultaneously being extensive among people who had the political, cultural, social and technological ability to pick up and relocate themselves as opportunity and circumstances dictated. The circumstances of when and why movements occurred is part

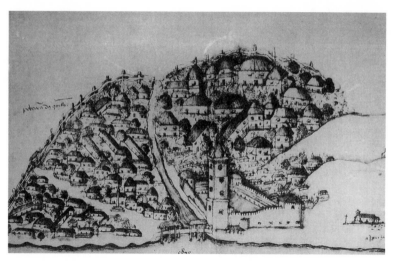

Malacca, *c.* 1536.

of the unrevealed detail of a history that defies conventional historical guidelines.

The history of Kuala Lumpur is intrinsically linked to the history of Malacca. Malacca is the last of the line of great trading centres of that era and its history demonstrates how the three major influences of the Indian Ocean world merge, interact and are absorbed into each other on the Malaysian peninsula. Malacca is a product of the Indianized world, a world that became Muslim as the city became Islamized, and then established its political and trading independence by establishing personal connection with China. These interactions did not begin with Malacca, nor did they end with the destruction of the Malacca sultanate by the Portuguese. The three distinctive strands of Kuala Lumpur society today have always been present, but they have undergone considerable reformulation thanks to the history of European colonization. Colonial history overlaid, reimagined and thereby reformulated incomprehension of the Malay world, making itself deaf to what the forests could tell, if the forests were consulted.

Malacca was not alone, a singularity on an otherwise empty and silent Malay peninsula, and its sway reached out to other

26

tributary states on Sumatra, whose history is deeply interwoven with that of the Malay peninsula. But Europe knew precious little of this reality when it stumbled into the Indian Ocean. The era of the European Renaissance, the age of 'discovery', in itself was dominated by recovery of classical Greek and Roman knowledge, and Greece and Rome knew little of what made the Indian Ocean world tick. The floodgates are conventionally said to have opened with the fall of Constantinople to the Ottoman Empire in 1453 when whole trunk-loads of lost Greek manuscripts were suddenly made available to Europe by fleeing Byzantines. Europe felt cut off and disadvantaged by the stranglehold Muslim civilization had on its access to the resources that made ordinary existence palatable: the spices such as pepper, cloves, nutmeg and cinnamon, and the luxuries it lusted after such as silk, carpets, cottons and so on. As standards of living and information improved in Europe it knew one thing very clearly: it had disastrous terms of trade with its nemesis, the Muslim world of the Middle East, with which it had been at loggerheads for centuries. So began the explorative ventures spearheaded by Portugal and Spain, the objective of which was to outflank the Muslim strongholds and find new allies beyond the Muslim lands. The great prize both nations sought was the fabled Spice Islands, reputedly somewhere in the vicinity of Cathay, as China was called. Columbus stumbled across America, thereby delaying Spanish arrival in the East Indies until Magellan's circumnavigation voyage of 1518–21. Magellan himself died in the Spice Islands of Indonesia, some of which he claimed for Spain. Portugal made it to India thanks to Vasco da Gama. The next item on the Portuguese agenda was to get from India to Malacca. So in 1506 an exultant King Manoel of Portugal despatched a mission to establish the headquarters of his empire of the Indies, which came to be Goa on the west coast of India, and then made a beeline for Malacca. By 1509 an expedition of four or five Portuguese ships weighed anchor off Malacca presenting credentials from Manoel and asking could they please come and trade. Such pettyfogging was not the temper Manoel's empire required. Enter the true spirit of European expansionism,

A Portuguese ship, *c.* 1595.

Portuguese in Malacca, *c.* 1595.

Afonso de Alberqueque, ubiquitous first viceroy of the Empire of India, who lost no time in beating a path to Malacca, laying siege, attacking and then destroying it after meeting determined resistance. The year was 1511, the precise moment a new round in European construction of forgetting begins in the Malay archipelago. So, let us remember what Tomas Pires, who sailed with Alberqueque, had to say of Malacca in his *Suma Oriental*, written between 1512 and 1515:

> Man cannot estimate the worth of Malacca on account of its greatness and profit, Malacca is a city that was made for merchandise, fitter than any other in the world; the end of monsoons and the beginning of others. Malacca is surrounded and lies in the middle, and the trade and commerce between different nations for a thousand leagues on every hand must come to Malacca.

The interesting thing is that once the Portuguese had hold of this jewel it became a spectre that somehow dematerialized in their hand; the golden legend that appeared at first glance so solid a reality became a *hantu*, a ghost, a *jinn* that disappeared back into the forest. They failed to realize the kind of profit from Malacca that the thriving city they conquered had commanded. Exactly the same fate befell the Dutch who from 1606, when they first attacked Portuguese Malacca, waged a decades-long campaign to gain control of the city. When the Dutch finally conquered Malacca in 1640 they too found that they could not gain much profit from the city they had set their hearts upon. The Dutch East India Company, with its headquarters in Batavia (the modern Jakarta) on Java, had to console itself with the knowledge that possession of Malacca was strategically essential, and quietly downgrade the city's position in the hierarchy of imperial administration. The Dutch East India Company was founded in 1602, two years after the Royal Charter of the Company of Merchants of London trading into the East Indies, otherwise known as the English East India Company. The London Company's first venture into the East Indies landed sick and soaked on Pulo (Pulau – island) Run in the Banda

Straits east of Java and the Celebes and nearly on the threshold of New Guinea. It took a long time for Europeans to learn that what Milton called 'the islands of spicerie' were actually located a long way beyond Malacca, Sumatra and Java. The Spice Islands were the Moluccas, home and only source of the clove. But cloves and all other spices were so widely traded around the Malay archipelago and Indian Ocean world that it was unnecessary to make the journey there unless the intention was to monopolize the market. Monopolizing the market was the aim of every European nation that ventured into the Indian Ocean, and they competed and fought with each other to establish their claims. In the process they disrupted and eventually succeeded in impoverishing the indigenous trading states so that Europe gained absolute control of the productive power of the region for its own uses. The doings of the Puritan Dutch in the 1640s were of intimate concern and interest to Puritan Englishmen. When Puritan Englishman came to power after the English Revolution of 1642–66, Oliver Cromwell even went to war with the Dutch to protect and forward the interests of the English East India Company. The leading intellectual of Cromwell's regime was one John Milton. So there is no surprise that Milton's Adam made special note of the Golden Chersonese when he surveyed the glories of all the world.

III

The rainforests, the repository of deep memory, have a very strong hold on the Malaysian imagination. Quite why this is so becomes clear when taking a walk into the forest at night. The moment the sun goes down, the forest comes alive with a veritable cacophony of sounds. The crickets begin to sing. The owls begin to hoot. The mosquitoes start to hover and whine. Countless male insects surge in unison, as though guided by a conductor, in clamorous and amorous clarion calls to expectant, reserved females. Near springs, or pools of water, the frogs – over a dozen different species – make a tremendous tumult. In this fit of acoustical madness, one can feel the menace in the whispering of the cool, lightly scented night breeze. The spine chills, as one notices that one is being observed – observed by countless eyes, of numerous sizes and colours, glowing in the dark, an intense gaze: the gaze of one who views you as an invader, a colonist, out on an unsavoury mission. The second one moves towards these twin coals of fire, they disappear – and then reappear again, elsewhere. Suddenly, there is a brilliant flash of colour from the spread of a stick insect or a beetle; but it disappears as soon as one notices it. Everything is still: but all is turbulence. The forest seems to be possessed, perhaps by the spirit of Majnun, left all alone after the death of Laila, reduced in his desolate agony to his linguistic root: jinn.

It is just as easy to believe that there are jinns and demons in the forest as it is to accept that there are black holes in the universe. In Menarah Indahh, tales of demons and jinns hovering in the forest abound. A jinn pair, Pongkol and his wife, come out at night and wile away their boredom by scaring the comfortable expatriates. For added fun, they practise lycanthrophy and transform themselves into forest animals. Then there is Hantu Penanggalan, a vampire demon who likes to float through the forest as a disembodied head complete with its intestines dangling below! Some jinns hunt other jinns: Hantu Pemburu is one of them; he is a huge leafy creature that stalks the forest at night looking for other demons. But not all jinns and demons are nasty. Tok Naning has a magnanimous disposition and warns people against forest diseases and venomous creatures such as snakes, scorpions, spiders and centipedes.

Jinns, being jinns, are also afflicted by the disease of postmodern fiction. Moyang Bojos is said to be a fierce man-eating creature, a combination of woman and machine, a true cyborg of bygone age. She is well endowed, and her right arm consists of a long, iron knife. But she is not very pretty, as her nostrils are upside down. So she is forced to take cover during storms, as the rain would flood into her nostrils and drown her. She was first seen by a pair of hunters looking for supper for their family. They saw a plump bird perched up a tree, took aim with their blowpipes and brought the game screaming to the ground. When they ran to pick it up, they saw, to their horror, that it landed right in front of a Bojos. They had to decide whether to run for their life empty-handed, or risk picking up the bird and being captured, even killed, by the Bojos. The envisioned hunger of their family got the better of them; and they tried, ever so gently, to pick up the bird without being noticed by the demon. But the Bojos caught them in her vice-like grip and took them prisoner. But she treated them well. She looked after them: when they ran out of tobacco she used her magic to turn hand-fuls of lichens into tobacco for them; when they were cold she lit a fire for them using Semut Api, the fire ants. Eventually, she even married one of them. One day, she said to the hunters: 'when you are out hunting and you hear the sound of a tree being chopped down, it is I who am cutting it down with my iron hand; but only those humans who are free from sin can see me'. She then disappeared. (It is not known whether she took her husband with her.) But even today, when brave men hear the sound of falling trees in the jungle in the middle of the night, they run for their lives.

IV

Why did Malacca become a *hantu*, a ghost of its former self, when conquered by the Portuguese? Why could the European powers, which vied for and possessed the city, not make Malacca as glorious under their administration as the Malay sultans had in their time? Why was its golden lure a will o' the wisp? The answer is fairly straightforward. It was not the city *per se* that generated the riches but the pervasive cultural acumen and way of life. Wealth could flow into and be concentrated in Malacca, when prevailing circumstances permitted. Or it could find a new level, make a new bend in the river or

It could be Laila, it could be Majnun – a Rajah Brooke's Birdwing butterfly.

Wayang kulit shadow-play puppets in a contemporary oil painting: Nik Zainal Abidin, *Wayang Kulit Kelantan*, 1965, oil on canvas.

Modern supermarket interior, Petaling Jaya.

Petaling Street – no longer negotiable.

Sultan Abdul Samad Building (the High Court), before the background was filled with high-rise buildings and traffic took over the square.

The art of gold weaving: an example of *Sankut*.

Ismail Mustam, *Hang Tuah and Hang Jebat*, 1961, oil on canvas.

The 'Arabian Nights' railway station.

The first building spree: KL's Moorish/Mughal administrative centre.

The latest building spree: overwriting Chinatown.

The ultimate status symbol: the Petronas 'Twin Towers'.

The Kuala Lumpur skyline before the new building boom of the '70s. The Tabang Hajji is the concave building to the far right.

round a further headland to another strategically located place on the Malay peninsula or Sumatra or Java as it had been doing for more than a millennium. The focus of empire and entrepot trade in the Malay archipelago has its importance. But the lasting significance is in the continuing vitality of inter-regional trade that was a constant feature of the Indian Ocean world irrespective of whichever great centres were in operation at any particular time. Europeans simply could not understand the ways of a world in which the apparent similarities occurred within such radical civilizational differences.

The sultans of the various states that emerged on the Malay peninsula stood at the head of a hierarchy. Their state and splendour came from charging taxes and levies on trade. So far that is just what Europeans would expect: it was after all exactly how European monarchs operated. The Malay Muslim sultans inherited aspects of a cultural tradition of their Indianized predecessors. In Indianized culture the king was a godhead, the city both a centre for trade and a ceremonial centre of religion and civilization. The regal colour was yellow and the person of the sovereign surrounded by much ritual and mystique, and, of course, one is not encouraged to be disloyal to a putative godhead. The greater the importance of the city, the more elaborate was the hierarchy of officials who surrounded the court of the sovereign. To this extent the Malay world paralleled Europe. Malacca had both a court hierarchy and a civil service hierarchy with all officials conscious of their status and position, and jealous in guarding their dignity and prerogatives. A major trading city would also have resident communities of foreigners, each of which would be grouped together and administer its own affairs according to its own law and custom under the aegis of a leading merchant. In Malacca there were Arab and various Indian and Chinese communities as well as peoples from other parts of the archipelago. The city was both the hub of its own flourishing civilization and cosmopolitan, open to the ideas and influences that came from near and far. The nature of the monsoon winds meant that trading delegations stayed in the cities for six months at a time, and when they left new delegations arrived for another six months from the opposite direction. It was this recurrent pattern of the gentle breezes that facilitated the peaceful spread of Islam through Southeast Asia. While many merchants just came and went, some stayed and founded families in the city. A striking instance are the Baba Nonyas of Malacca, the Chinese community that, while still distinctly Chinese, has over the generations also become discernibly Malaysian, speaking Malay and adopting specific forms of Malay dress. The Baba Nonya have Bumi status within the modern state of Malaysia, that is, recognition as 'sons of the soil' or original members of the modern Malaysian polity.

To become an Eastern emporium of entrepot trade any city had to command a large surplus in foodstuffs from local trade to victual the foreign merchants who remained for long periods of time. The bedrock of extensive foreign trade was local trade. And long distance and local were interconnected with regional trade in the spices that made Southeast Asia famous. This meant that knowledge of long-distance trade was widely spread throughout the region. So when for some reason, such as crop failure, drought, disease or political trouble in the hinterland, a city faced problems, a new trading city would emerge in another location and, by the services and convenience it offered to the traders from afar, begin its rise in prominence. Malacca was not rich and glorious because it was the source of a specific product. Its glory was founded on its openness and hospitality, the service it rendered to the ceaseless stream of peoples who were constituent parts of its *convivencia*; this was an art, a skill, which Europeans neither recognized nor knew how to approximate. When they took control they set about regulating all trade, local, regional and long distance. The Portuguese insisted that the Indian Ocean was a closed sea under their sole administration. All traders must go immediately to a port prescribed by the Portuguese to obtain a licence, pay their duties and then go about their business under the watchful eye of the well-armed Portuguese galleons, the men of war. Everything was lost in this translation. The subtlety that interconnected a world of civilizations sought to seep through the gaps and maintain itself about the edges of this unsophisticated extortion racket.

A sultan was nothing without a city. The city and its sultan were nothing without a hinterland. It was the system of treaties and tribute, local and regional interconnections, ceremonially encrusted but carrying specific political and pragmatic meaning that built the prestige of the city and the sultan. As the Portuguese set about establishing their inflexible control from Malacca, the ousted sultan escaped into the forest. It was not only Malays of the peninsula who determinedly resisted the Portuguese. In 1513 a massive Javanese fleet headed for Malacca to oust the interlopers, but sea power – the huge and well-armed European vessels – were the hinge of empire. The Javanese fleet was destroyed at sea. The resistance of Indian Ocean states to European encroachment comprised not only open warfare. Defiance also consisted in the continuing attempt to evade the arbitrary restrictions and impositions of each and every European power that ventured into the area. Acheh in northern Sumatra became a focus for much of the trade that quitted Malacca rather than submit to the Portuguese. The relocated Malacca sultanate became the sultanate of Johore and sought to recapture its former glory and trade. So the fabled city became a ghost and European powers, despite all their presumption, had to attempt to learn the ropes of local trading if they were to turn a profit. While European trade was for a long time only gnat bites on the prosperity of the Indian Ocean world, the die had been cast. An infallible connection existed in the European mind between trade and military domination, along with the unquestioned assumption of superior rights to do and dispose solely according to their own interests and concerns. This new ethos, rather than adding to the prosperity of the whole region, led to a 'beggar the Others, the locals' mentality that was the meaning of colonial domination.

Once European power established itself in the Indian Ocean, conventional history is concerned almost exclusively with their internecine activities, on the presumption that they were bound to dominate. So it constructs forgetting of and indifference to the activities of the indigenous states of the Malay peninsula and the entire region. Since 'We' are here 'They' must be irrelevant seems to be the implicit thesis. The sultans and their cities, indeed the entire extensive cultural system bound to trade, did not cease. The record of Other history is there for those who would consult it and displays the disruption visited on the Malay world by the double bind of trying to oppose and defy European interference. In the end, this increasingly intrusive system compounded the worst failings of the indigenous states and opened the way for further inroads by colonizing European powers. Colonialism lacked the spirit and temper of the older Indian Ocean world; the new order it constructed resolutely refused to learn from the openness and cosmopolitan values of the original, indigenous environment. The effort to relocate and re-establish relationships among indigenous states caused dissension and vying for power in an ever-widening ripple effect. To this must be added the internal disruptions that were a regular part of their working. Malay sultans were elected from among suitable candidates of the royal house by the local chiefs and *penghulus*, the leading citizens of the villages. In many states a potential sultan was expected to serve in a hierarchy of posts that enabled him to be known to and gain the confidence of the chiefs and *penghulu* before ascending the throne. Conflicts over succession, however, were a common feature of the history of all Malayan states. They could last a few years or even decades and generate civil wars, cause migrations between states and lead to the founding of new ones.

The eighteenth century saw the arrival of the Bugis on the Malay peninsula. The Bugis originate from southern Celebes, around the area of Macassar. For years the Macassar Bugis resisted the monopoly the Dutch sought to impose on the clove trade with the island of Ceram. Their activities, of course, were termed piracy by the Dutch, themselves the arch-pirates. In 1660 the Sultan of Macassar was forced to sign a treaty promising to stop trading with Ceram. Seven years later, when the trade had not ceased, the Dutch conquered and garrisoned Macassar. Four months later, in 1668, they deposed the sultan and made Macassar a subject territory under a Dutch governor. This lead to a wholesale relocation of Bugis who dispersed through Java, Sumatra, the Malay peninsula and beyond. The Bugis were fierce warriors who had the habit of fighting in suits of chain mail, an idea they had acquired from observing the Portuguese, an early and successful form of technology transfer. It was thus natural for the sultans who ruled the Malay peninsula to ask the Bugis to join them as paid soldiers. In return the Bugis demanded the creation of a new position, a kind of under-kingship, for themselves; they further secured their position by marriages with local princesses. Soon, the sultans discovered that the Bugis had an upper hand, effectively making them puppet rulers. A succession struggle in the northern Malaysian state of Kedah was won by the candidate who recruited Bugis forces. The unfortunate sultan discovered he was doubly beholden to them: not only for his position but also, being unable to pay them, as their debtor as well. By about 1680

The burning of a Bugis stronghold on the Johore coast by Dutch East India Company troops, 1784.

Bugis had begun to settle around the valleys of the Klang River and River Selangor; and by the 1740s the state of Selangor was asserting its independence under a Bugis ruler.

v

Selangor is the state in which Kuala Lumpur is located, but it was more than a century after the founding of the state that its eventual premier city came into existence. And it was a considerable time after the emergence of Kuala Lumpur before the sultan's capital was moved there from the coastal city of Klang. Everything about the beginnings of Kuala Lumpur was somewhat off-centre of the city itself. To understand Kuala Lumpur one has to see it in the context of the history of the region as a whole. To come to know what makes KL distinctive, one has to know Malay life and Malaysian history. As the capital city of an independent nation Kuala Lumpur has gathered into itself all the strands of which Malay life and Malaysian history is composed and reflects, more than anywhere else in Malaysia, all the consequences, effects, contradictions and conundrums of a modern nation. Kuala Lumpur is the Wilaya Perskutuan, the Federal Territory, in which and from which the whole of Malaysia is made. Little more than a century ago it was jungle; it was made by Malaysian history and today makes the course of Malaysia's future. The city stands pre-eminent, but it does not, cannot, stand alone.

Ampang, where I live, is actually where Kuala Lumpur began. The first tin mine, now an artificial lake, which sparked the growth of the city, is visible from my balcony at Menarah Indahh. The lake is just behind the modestly named Ampang Mini Market, a cornucopia of all the tasty goods for which the relocated palettes of diverse expatriates hunger as well as the delicacies of all the local cuisines, Malay, Chinese and Indian. As such, I consider the Mini Market a vestige of the indigenous reality of the trading world of Southeast Asia. To shop there is

46

Java Street, Kuala Lumpur, *c.* 1884.

an act of deference to local history. From my balcony I can take in the beginning, the growth and present-day burgeoning of Kuala Lumpur, through time and in space.

In the middle of the nineteenth century, when this place was nothing but jungle, prospectors could travel upstream on the Klang River, from the coastal capital, to where it met the River Gombak. At the junction of the rivers now stands the Mesjid Jamek, the most elegant mosque in KL. From there onwards the waterway was too narrow and shallow for the use of boats, and prospectors had to hack their way through thick jungle. What brought them was the age-old Malaysian export, tin. In 1857, the year when all of India rose up against the British Raj, two rajahs of Selangor launched an expedition to prospect for tin in the area. Rajah Juma'at, who knew a thing or two about mining, persuaded his brother, Rajah Abdullah, chief of the ancient capital of Klang, to send a party of prospectors upriver to Ampang. Within four weeks of their arrival, 69 of the original 87 miners

47

had died of malaria. But the lure of Ampang was too much to deter the rajahs. Shortly afterwards, they organized another party of 150 miners to venture into the jungle. This time they had better luck. Perhaps this was because the Chinese miners, superstitious as they are said to have been, took with them a group of Malay magicians or *pawangs*. The *pawangs* provided the miners with certain rules for success: no umbrellas in the opencast mines; no shoes either. Eventually, tin began to float down river by boat. The trickle increased, becoming commercially viable. As serious profits appeared on the horizon, the mining settlement of Ampang began to take shape. Contrary to the received impression of conventional history of modern Malaya, the beginnings of Kuala Lumpur owe their inspiration to the long-established pattern of enterprise of the Malays. One can read a considerable number of history books and still not learn that Malays had been mining tin for millennia. The arrival of tin mining is supposedly an invention of the British Empire and Chinese immigrant labour. Ampang contradicts that fiction, in the sense that it looks back and refers to the old world of the Indian Ocean that predates and is submerged in a new era of

Capitan Cina Yap Ah Loy in full splendour to right of centre, among a group of administrators, Kuala Lumpur, *c.* 1884.

colonial overwriting. Two years after the opening of the Ampang mine, two Chinese businessmen, Hiu Siew and An Sze Keledek, set up a trading post at the river junction, on the right-hand side of the river, near the tracks to the mines. It would have been about where the Central Market now stands in Kuala Lumpur. Hiu Siew is said to have been a man of unusual ability and acumen. He impressed Rajah Abdullah enough to be appointed the first head of the Chinese community; the title 'Capitan Cina' first occurs in Portuguese records of their administration of Malacca – the system of distinct communities regulating themselves is an ancient part of the Indian Ocean world.

The Malay world built predominantly and often exclusively in wood, leaving few if any monuments, so its history was constantly reintegrating with the forests. This environmental constant compounds the talent for forgetting of conventional history. What it cannot see it cannot date and therefore cannot comprehend or imagine. Conventional history looks at KL from the perspective of the toeholds of British imperialism on the coast, inland to the impenetrability of a silent and undisturbed forest. The beginnings of Ampang and Kuala Lumpur remain marginal for quite sometime to the Rafflesian developments around the fringes of the peninsula. So long as Malaya was a colony, KL was a backwater concerned with the doings of upcountry planters, odd types who often times turn odder due to the influence of the jungle, like characters in the Somerset Maugham stories. From the Rafflesian perspective, it was Chinese *towkays* in the Straits Settlements, in particular Singapore but also Penang and Malacca, who were the crucial factor in the development of tin mining in Malaya. These *towkays* were newly immigrant Chinese businessmen whose merchant capital effectively opened the way for British imperialism and the rich rewards it eventually reaped from Malaya.

Though newly arrived and most convenient to imperialist ends, the Chinese immigrants did not escape the Orientalist gaze. The miners relied heavily upon each other, in particular through the formation of *kongsi*, the Chinese concept of partnership, social

solidarity and economic growth. *Kongsi* literally means government by the general public. In mainland China, it became the
focus of a famous 1455 rebellion led by Teng Mao-Chi who established *kongsi* as a new way of life based on equality and partnership. In the Klang valley, it became the reason for a number
of Chinese uprisings, as the mining settlements became entan-
gled in or reacted to the volatile political affairs of the Malay
States. The main function of *kongsi* was to establish the mining
communities with their own resources and to ensure the economic growth of the community. In this they succeeded consid-
erably. British administrators and British history have a
particularly murky view of the *kongsi*. As if observing an inex-
plicable mystery of the Oriental character, they note the arrival
of rival Chinese secret societies in the tin mining settlements
around Ampang. They blame the societies for inevitably pro-
ducing intercommunity strife and exploitation of the very

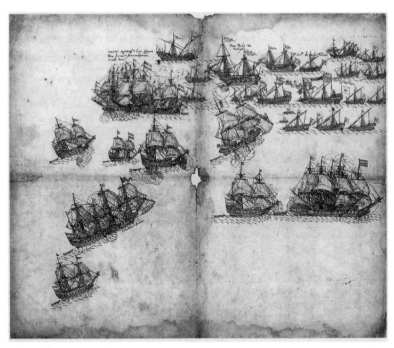

Portuguese and Dutch East India Company ships skirmish off the coast of Malacca,
c. 1606.

miners the partnerships were supposed to protect, while usually ignoring the other functions they performed that gave essential support to migrant workers in a strange environment. The fertile imagination of the Orientalist gaze expresses itself through emotive language. These secret societies recruited, represented and combined Chinese from different parts of China who spoke different languages. What so irked the British administrators was the fact that members of the societies were sworn to secrecy; breaking the oath meant a certain death. There were also elaborate initiation rites, secret signs and absolute loyalty to leaders. It made the tough miners into effective fighting forces when occasion arose. It also meant that all the members of the entire community from the humblest miner to the *towkay* were part of an inclusive organization, not free-floating individuals to be marshalled according to British rules, regulations and desires. Kuala Lumpur had two main secret societies. Hai San, the secret society that controlled Kuala Lumpur proper, known after the five districts area of South China where it originated, consisted of members who spoke Hakka or Hokkien. It was constantly involved in bitter fights with Ghi Hin, known after its area of origin, the four districts. Ghi Hin dominated the nearby township of Kanching and its members were predominantly Cantonese speakers. The offences of these Chinese secret societies are exactly paralleled by those of the friendly societies established by industrial workers in Britain. The taking of secret oaths was the precise offence that led to the transportation of the Tolpuddle Martyrs. The ethos of friendly societies and *kongsi* are markedly similar. To see one as the ancestor of modern trade unionism and the other as a secret society redolent of the world of Fu Manchu introduces an impenetrable demarcation, a world of incomprehension.

The Malay and Chinese communities that created Kuala Lumpur worked side by side, the Chinese mines running alongside Malay agriculture, each settled in their own quarters. The Malays separated themselves from the Chinese, because as Muslims they would not live near pigs, which the Chinese

51

raised for meat, and anyway it was part of an ancient pattern of discrete but interactive existence that had always operated in this part of the world. The boundary between the communities was Java Street, now Jalan Tun Perak, the main road running through the Chinatown district. The boundary could become a line of friction. Things came to a head in the late 1860s. In 1868, Yap Ah Loy was appointed Capitan Cina of both Kuala Lumpur and Kanching. As he was a newcomer to the region, his appointment was bitterly contested both by ordinary Chinese traders and by powerful businessmen. Born in 1837, Yap was a Hakka who arrived penniless in Malacca at the age of seventeen. Shrewd, highly intelligent and quite ruthless when required, Yap became the most powerful man in the Chinese community within a period of fourteen years. Yap's appointment came when a Malay civil war that had rippled out to involve the Chinese miners was coming to its denouement. The miners had lost faith in the Malay viceroy, Tunku Kudin, an ally of Yap. They joined Kudin's enemies, Rajah Mahdi, Rajah Mahmud and Syed Mashhur, to fight against him and his European mercenaries, during which Kuala Lumpur was burnt to the ground. For a relatively new city Kuala Lumpur has risen from devastation numerous times. The reality of the city is that it is always being remade, as I have observed from my balcony. Yap fled, but returned later to a devastated city, a mirror of the personal history of innumerable Malay sultans.

However, Kuala Lumpur's fortunes began to improve towards the end of 1870s. When Sultan Abdul Samad of Selangor came to visit the city in 1879, the local Malays welcomed him with open arms. It was a show of loyalty that found favour with the sultan, who decided to make Kuala Lumpur the capital of the state. So the following year, the state capital moved from the ancient town of Klang to Kuala Lumpur. The British, who had been in the Malaya for over a hundred years, established in Singapore, Malacca and Penang, also began to take notice of the new capital city. The first British Resident was appointed in Selangor in 1784; in March 1880, he was transferred from Klang to Kuala Lumpur.

VI

The backwater of Kuala Lumpur came into being off-centre and out of sight of the reformulation underway around the coasts of Malaysia. The chief architect of the reformulation that was to keep Kuala Lumpur a secondary, upcountry place until after independence was Thomas Stamford Raffles. He began his career as a teenager working as a clerk for the East India Company in London. Since its foundation in 1600 the English East India Company had made repeated attempts to capitalize on the 'islands of spicerie' but were continually losing out to the better-established Portuguese and Dutch operations. So John Company, as it was familiarly known, concentrated on India. At the end of the eighteenth century, when all of Europe was embroiled in turmoil stemming from the French Revolution and the Napoleonic Wars, a new window of opportunity appeared to open in the East Indies. The United Provinces (Holland) had been overrun and an administration in exile was operating from London. Jan Campaigne, the Dutch East India Company, was hardly in a position to rebuff the manoeuvring of its London rival. In 1795 a British garrison took over the defence of Malacca under an agreement with the Dutch government. A decade earlier, the British merchant Francis Light had convinced the East India Company to open a factory at Penang with himself as the superintendent. His appointment was a reward for having secured a treaty with the Sultan of Kedah, which transferred possession of the island of Penang to the British, who immediately renamed the island after the Prince of Wales. There was a great deal of indecision about what to do with Penang, not least because the initial agreement had called for the Sultan of Kedah to receive military aid for his internal problems; the aid never arrived, causing him to ask for his island back. In 1805 the East India Company decisively changed its mind and instead of leaving Penang as a one-man outfit, despatched a whole body of administrative personnel to convert the place into a presidency. Young Raffles was one of these new administrators. Then it occurred to headquarters in

India that they might as well abandon Malacca and move everyone to their new presidency in Penang. It so happened that when this idea was floated Raffles was on sick leave in Malacca, and he wrote a report detailing the nature of local Southeast Asian trade which made possession of the port a continuing necessity. This report brought him to the attention of Lord Minto, governor general in India, who then appointed Raffles as 'Agent to the Governor for the Malay States'. The position meant that Raffles was a combination of intelligence agent and diplomat. One gets a fair idea of how he saw his job because his other idea was that the British should use their bases in Malaya to launch an invasion of Java. Both Raffles and Lord Minto sailed with the invasion fleet. History makes Raffles a charismatic figure, a real Enlightenment man. He wrote books on the history, human and natural, of the region, collected vast quantities of its material culture and samples of its flora and fauna which, unfortunately, ended up at the bottom of the sea when the ship carrying them back to Britain foundered. He learnt to speak Malay, his teacher being Munshi Abdullah, the author of the *Hikayat Abdullah*. The Munshi seems to have liked Raffles, which leads a lot of Malays to regard the former as something of a quisling, or first in the line of colonized clones and captive minds. Nevertheless, Malaysian school children are force-fed the *Hikayat Abdullah* as a kind of foundational classic. The Enlightenment was the great era of Orientalism; in keeping with its general habits, Raffles used what he learnt of Malay culture to facilitate the construction of knowledgeable ignorance. The eminent scholarship of Raffles and many of the colonial administrators that came after him effectively became a kind of forgetting that made Malays marginal to the history of their own lands, that kept them on the fringes of the new colonial order Raffles created for and bequeathed to Malaya.

When the Napoleonic Wars ended, the Dutch were anxious to get back their possessions. The Treaty of Utrecht began making the kind of clean lines of spheres of influence that colonialism came to relish. Within a few years what is now Indonesia was marked exclusively in the Dutch column and the whole of the Malay peninsula in the British. While this arrangement was being worked out Raffles was still working as an intelligence officer, but stationed at the only British outpost left in Indonesia. This was Bencoolen on the south coast of Sumatra. Bencoolen was a real backwater, well off the beaten track, from which the company had signally failed to realize a profit. Raffles, however, set about trying to make his mark, establishing pepper and coffee plantations and fulminating about the awfulness of the Dutch treatment of the locals. His particular objection was slave labour; his solution, to man his new plantations with transported convict Indians, had insidious implications. The convicts were no freer than slaves and they marginalized the locals even further, making them irrelevant to the actual operations and control of colonial production. The pattern persisted and became pervasive and could be called the Rafflesian legacy to Malaya. His strategic intelligence activities, however, were not at an end. His great achievement was to note the prime location and arrange for the acquisition of the island of Singapore from the Sultan of Johore, facilitated by internal machinations within the state. He framed the rules and regulations which marked how Britain administered its newly created colony, the pre-eminent of what were known as the Straits Settlements, that is, Singapore, Penang and Malacca.

The doyen of British historians of the region, Richard Winstedt, announces in his *Malaya and Its History*, 'The history of Singapore is written mainly in statistics' – a prescient phrase, I always think, since the tradition is assiduously maintained by the island state even today. Once established, Singapore became the crucial link in Britain's parody of the ancient Indian Ocean trading world. It was a major hub of the new colonial world system by which Britain came to dominate India, its interests in Southeast Asia and trade to China. It was a macabre, dark-side antithesis of the indigenous original. The East India Company made Singapore an obligatory port of call for all ships trading to China. Today any air traveller arriving in Malaysia or Singapore will be informed in precise language that drug trafficking is a serious crime, punishable by death. Both countries have good reason for their policies. China produced tea, and before they smuggled the technology of tea production to India the East India Company was laying out a lot of money to buy tea in China, being unable to find goods the Chinese were anxious to buy. India, however, produced abundant crops of opium and thus was born a stratagem emulated by modern tobacco companies. Addict the Chinese to opium and the terms of the tea trade suddenly became immensely profitable for the East India Company. Until Hong Kong was invented in 1848, all ships bound for China had to pass through Singapore, where, en route, profit could be made by selling opium to the new wave of Chinese immigrants being attracted to the Straits Settlements. The blame for this weakness was firmly laid on the Oriental character and not on the East India Company, which created the itch, scratched it, made enormous profits from it and then roundly condemned it.

The British had an insatiable desire for the economic wealth of Malaya. But it took a considerable time to find the right keys to unlocking it. Plantations of tropical produce of various kinds made their appearance before Malaysia became the apotheosis of all extraction colonies with the introduction of rubber. The ecological story of Empire is the transportation of crops from one side of the world to another, the displacement and over-writing of nature as much as of people, which often added its own increment to the catastrophic impact of colonial domination. As they worked away at making a profit, the British were not very keen on installing an extensive administration throughout the Malaya peninsula as the thick jungles and their dreaded inhabitants presented problems. The administrative centres were the Straits Settlements; their garrisons, police force and civil servants were imported from India, as were plantation workers. The Straits Settlements were bridgeheads; securing them required a measure of intelligence and control over the affairs of the mainland of the peninsula, especially those areas in which increasingly lucrative tin mining was taking place. The stratagem that worked so well in India was simply applied to the Malay States. The sultans were required to accept a British Resident, just as the rajahs in India had been. Theoretically, the Residents were there to 'advise', but, as the treaties made clear, once they were in place their advice was not only to be given, it was to be followed. Various permutations on the system applied, but the Resident's prime directive was to render the 'advice' that would make the Malay States compliant with the needs of British colonialism and so reorganize the administration of the states as to make them comprehensible to the British. After extensive negotiations, it was agreed in 1874 that the states of Perak and Selangor would accept a British 'Resident'. The following year, residents also made themselves comfortable in Negri Sembilan and Pahang. A demarcation was made between the modern reorganization under the aegis of the Resident and Malay religion and custom, which was left to the sultans and their traditional system. This was exactly the same *cordon sanitaire* that had been employed in India, and in both places it had markedly similar results. An enclave of modernity was superimposed upon a world of tradition that was reconstituted as old, outmoded, inimical and by its very nature inferior.

It is not always easy, however, to separate custom and tradition from economic and political concerns. So the Residents had to manoeuvre carefully, ensuring British interests were served without upsetting the natives or their sultans or insulting their customs or traditions. Most Residents accomplished this feat reasonably well. However, a certain James Birch, the first Resident of Perak, managed to commit the ultimate crime in the Malay book of customs. He made Sultan Abdullah lose face. So early one sunny November morning in 1875, Birch, who had arrived in the village of Pasar Saleh to post orders announcing that the kingdom of Perak was to be governed by British officers from now on, headed for a refreshing bath. At the palmleaf bathhouse on the riverbank he met a group of men running 'amok'. One struck the Resident in the head with a sword and the river did the rest. The British thought that a major uprising was brewing in Perak and summoned soldiers and marines from India and Hong Kong. But when the heavily equipped army marched into Perak, it met with no resistance. Honour had been avenged, the culprit punished. There was no need to fight the British.

'Wait a minute; is this how it really happened in history?'

This question, asked by an actor who has just stepped out of character, is the central motif of Kee Thuan Chye's playful play 'We Could **** You Mr Birch', produced by the nascent theatre workshop of KL. There is a close relationship between myth and history, representation and drama. Myths shape history and turn representation into drama. Representations generate myths but are often presented as history. When the best drama translates representation, it seeks to subvert and reveal its mythical character. Kee's drama seeks to displace British representation of Malaysians and their history with a more questioning inter-

Frank Swettenham, Resident of Selangor, Governor Malay Straits Settlement, later High Commissioner of the Federated Malay States, 1901–4.

The Perak River near Kuala Kangsar, 1897, where Captain James Birch was supposed to have been killed in 1875.

pretation. He uses the narrative of the imperial past to raise a number of questions about the colonial presence in Malaysia, whimsically weaving the theatre of the absurd with overtones of Brecht, subverting both the dominant (colonial) historical discourse and modern Malaysian politics. The play within the play is in rehearsal. And actors frequently step out of character to question the narrative they are supposedly representing. The subversive questioning starts right at the beginning. This is the dialogue between two actors playing historical roles:

> 'History? What history? We are creating fiction, Yatim [real name of the actor]. This is fiction. History is fiction.'
> 'What about historical truth, Mano?'
> 'Truth depends on who is telling the history and what he is trying to get across, who his audience are. History can even be manipulated to convey opposing truths. You can screw around with history, lah!'

'So how do we tell what is the real truth?'

'Now you know of course that the man sent to be British Resident of Perak was James W. W. Birch.'

'Yes, that is historically true.'

'Listen to what his colleague Frank Swettenham wrote about him. [He produces a book and reads from it.] "In Mr Birch the British Government lost one of its most courageous, able and zealous officers." Is this absolute truth? How about this? [He produces another book.] Written by his successor, Sir Hugh Low: "Birch was violent, drunk, and did some high-handed things." Hmm, is this true too?'

But it is not merely the representation of Birch that is at issue here. Of greater concern is the representation of different communities in Malaysia and how these representations have been internalized by Malaysians themselves. We are given a hint of that representation when we first meet Birch in the play:

60

They came to Kuala Lumpur from *kampung* like these throughout the peninsula.

'There is much to be made from this place. A lot of tin to be turned into gold in the booming market. Otherwise why would the British Crown be interested in intervening in the local affairs? I'm not sent here as a British Resident to restore peace and order for altruistic reasons. Yet even so, these locals are incapable of organizing themselves. What they know best is fighting. For gain. The upriver chiefs versus the downriver chiefs. And the bloody Chinamen and their rival secret societies. Drop a gold shilling and they can hear it miles away. No one can be trusted. I will have to see that the revenues from taxes goes into the right coffers. From now on government officials will have to take the responsibility of collecting revenue. The local chiefs will no longer be trusted with that. Not much would be left by the time it had passed through their hands.'

The *kampung* that became the city: the environs of Kuala Lumpur *c.* 1884.

The representation of Malays and Chinese that acquired truly mythical proportion, and has become an integral part of Malaysian history, is largely due to Frank Swettenham. He was the Resident of Selangor and later became the high commissioner of the Federated Malay States, as the areas that accepted Residents came to be collectively known. In his works, *The Real Malay* and *Malay Sketches*, completed in 1885 and 1899 respectively, Swettenham created portraits of Malays that came to define the Malay character. 'The leading characteristic of the Malay of every class', he suggested, 'is a disinclination to work.' Like other Muslims of Orientalist lore, the Malay was also fatalistic and superstitious. But above all else, 'he is conservative to a degree, is proud and fond of his country and his people, venerates his ancient customs and traditions, fears his Rajas, and has a proper respect for constituted authority – while he looks askance on all innovations and will resist their sudden introduction'. Swettenham suggested an environmental reason for the Malay laziness: 'Less than one month's fitful exertion in twelve, a fish basket in the river or in a swamp, an hour with a casting net in the evening, would supply a man with food. A little more than this and he would have something to sell.

62

Probably that accounts for the Malay's inherent laziness; that and a climate which inclines the body to ease and rest, the mind to dreamy contemplation rather than to strenuous and persistent toil. It is, however, extremely probable that the Malay's disinclination to exert himself is also due to the fact that, in the course of many generations, many hundreds of years, he has learned that when he did set his mind and his body moving, and so acquired money or valuables, these possessions immediately attracted the attention of those who felt that they could make a better use of them than the owner.' But even though he was 'unquestionably opposed to steady continuous work', the Malay could be persuaded to a certain kind of work: 'if you can only give him an interest in the job, he will perform prodigies: he will strive, and endure, and be cheerful and courageous with the best. Take him on the war-path or any kind of chase, or even on some prosaic expedition which involves travel by river, or sea, or jungle, something therefore which has a risk: then the Malay is thoroughly awake, and you wish for no better servant, no more pleasant or cheery companion. Perhaps it is these qualities which, a hundred years ago, made him such a dreaded pirate.' But why did he lack initiative? Swettenham offers the following explanation: 'there was, in 1874, a very broad line indeed between the ruling classes in Malaya and the *raiats*, the people. The people had no initiative whatever; they were there to do what their chiefs told them – no more, no less. They never thought whether anything was right or wrong, advantageous to them personally or otherwise; it was simply, "What is the Rajah's order?" Wherever the Rajah was recognized his order ran; the only exception would be where some local chief defied or disputed the authority of the Rajah and told the people that they were only to take orders from him. Such a case would happen but seldom.' This is a true piece of hypocrisy from a Resident whose very *raison d'être* was to be He Who Shall Be Obeyed.

In contrast to the Malays, the Chinese were perceived as industrious and hard-working but inclined to duplicity. 'They smoke opium, they lie without restraint, and whenever opportunity offers are dishonest, cunning, and treacherous', wrote a British traveller, but once they are restricted by British law from these activities, they 'are the most useful and most indispensable members of society'. As the Malay sociologist, Syed Hussein Alatas, brother of the al-Attas who dated the Trengganu Stone, has shown in his classic study, *The Myth of the Lazy Native*, these representations were a function of the role the natives performed in empire building. The Malays worked, and worked hard; otherwise they could not survive. They sowed their fields, went downriver to fish, built and maintained their houses and carried out the everyday chores of a farming community. But they were quite unwilling 'to become a tool in the production system of colonial capitalism'. Moreover, they were largely rural people and did not come in contact with the Europeans, who confined themselves to urban areas. The Malays were represented as lazy because they were self-sufficient and refused to work as slave labour, which the Chinese were coerced into doing because of their immigrant status. The Chinese, on the other hand, supplied the British with all their worldly comforts: they served as house servants, bar tenders, built roads and rail-

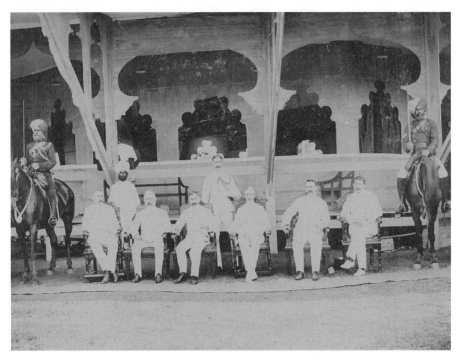

Empire on display: the High Commissioner and residents, Kuala Lumpur, 1903.

ways, mined ores and did the necessary clerical estate work. In other words, they were trapped into the most degrading kind of domestic, mining and estate labour. The Malays performed no useful function in the contours of colonial capitalism; the Chinese were an integral part in its expansion. When the Malays did enter colonial capitalism, they worked in the state administration of the sultans. This work was largely hidden from the ordinary colonial gaze and therefore went unappreciated.

VII

Imperialism considered the colonies to be unwilling but desirable brides. The Malay annals themselves tell numerous stories of unwilling brides, lost and won, fought over and fought with. One tale tells of the daughter of Seri Nara Diraja, a noble at the court of Sultan Mahmud. During a visit to Malacca by Pateh Adam, the ruler of Surabaya, the Nara Diraja's two-year-old daughter, Tun Manda, played with the ruler and whispered something in his ear. Jokingly Nara Diraja said that the little girl was proposing to him. 'Then I accept', said the Javanese prince. When Tun Manda reached marriageable age, Pateh Adam returned to Malacca to collect the bride he thought had been promised. He came with forty nobles and numerous warriors. But Nara Diraja remembered nothing and said it must have been only a joke. Furious, Pateh Adam decided to abduct Nara Diraja's daughter. A violent fight broke out during which Pateh Adam caught the girl, and holding his *kris*, the ornate dagger, to her throat, threatened to kill her unless she married him. The poor girl, having no choice, consented. Seri Nara Diraja also had to give in to Pateh Adam's demands. Pateh Adam returned to Surabaya with his unwilling bride.

The colonial conquests of peninsular Malaya followed a similar narrative. So by the time the Victorian explorer, Isabella Bird, arrived in Selangor in 1879, just after the civil war, still unmarried, and just turned 47, she looked at Malaya as a handmaiden, dirty, troublesome but with some desirable features. 'Selangor', she wrote in her travelogue, *The Golden Chersonese*, 'is bounded on the north by the "protected" State of Perak, which became notorious in England a few years ago for a "little war" in which we inflicted a very heavy chastisement on the Malays for the assassination of Mr Birch, the British Resident.' She didn't think that Selangor had much of a future: 'Selangor thrives, if it does thrive, which I greatly doubt, on tin and gotta.' The Klang valley was 'a most mis-thriven, decayed, dejected, miserable looking place'. But she was impressed by 'Kwala Lumpor': a 'true capital, created by the enterprise of Chinamen'. Isabella Bird epitomizes the new outlook of Empire, a writer whose display of superficial knowledge masks her dissemination of a new layer of Western ignorance. She recycles the phrase Golden Chersonese, properly attributed to both Ptolemy and Milton, only to announce unequivocally on the first page: 'the

OXFORD IN ASIA PAPERBACKS

ISABELLA L. BIRD

THE

GOLDEN CHERSONESE

TRAVELS IN MALAYA IN 1879

Malay Peninsula of our day has no legitimate claim to an ancient history.' This is nonsense, of course, but amazingly still accepted as scholarly truth by a majority of Malaysians.

When Frank Swettenham became Resident of Selangor he realized that the new capital city was in urgent need of a facelift. The old town was thus pulled down street by street, old huts were replaced with brick houses and shops and narrow streets were transformed into wide thoroughfares. It is part of the fate of Kuala Lumpur that travellers arrive when it is undergoing rebuilding. The contemporary *bon mot* is the local joke that Malaysia's national bird is the crane – the mechanical kind that dot the skyline visible from my balcony, urgently engaged in raising some new structure. Each new building replaces a patch of forest or field or older habitation and thus erases the past. Soon after Swettenham's arrival, streets were lit with kerosene lamps and work began on the famous Lake Gardens, an extensive park, then on the edges of the city. When the British governor of the Straits Settlement, Governor Weld, visited Kuala Lumpur in 1886, he found it a neat and pretty Malay and Chinese town. Yet it still seemed a provincial place when compared to Singapore. It was still deep in the jungle, inland and isolated.

The most crowded part of the city was Chinatown, spread along the east bank of the Klang River. An indigenous form of architectural art evolved here in form of shop-houses. The buildings had narrow fronts, but were very deep. They were set back at least five feet from the streets to allow space for covered pavements, known as *kaki lima*. The front of the buildings was almost always open, housing the shop and also allowing air to circulate freely. The upper levels projected forward to cover the pavements. The windows were shuttered to let air in and keep the sun out. At the back, there was space for a lane, parallel with the street front, used by bullock carts collecting nightsoil and, in case of emergencies, the fire brigade. All the

The Selangor Club, a.k.a. The Spotted Dog, 1903 – complete with cricket pitch and sight screen.

shop-houses were decorated with mock pillars and artwork known as 'Chinese Rococo'. The shop-houses are disappearing fast; those that remain are crumbling and encrusted with the excreta of modernity, neon signs and fast food boards. Kuala Lumpur is only toying with the Singaporean fashion, the yup-pification of the few remaining examples. In Singapore, they are turned into trendy upmarket shops or offices but especially restaurants that serve anything but local fare. The most notable renovations in KL house fast food restaurants offering burgers, fried chicken or pizza. In Kuala Lumpur you can still get glimpses of the elegance and beauty of these buildings, but you have to peer up, around and behind the detritus.

By 1891, the production of tin had increased over fivefold since Yap Ah Loy's time. The opening of the Suez Canal in 1869 had been a great aid, enabling firmer incorporation of Malayan produce into the industrial economy of Britain. By this time the mechanization of tin mining through the introduction of steam-powered dredging had transformed the ownership and financing of the industry. The large capital investment in mechanization was more than the Chinese could cope with and European com-panies inherited the enterprise they had not pioneered. The legacy of this transfer is memorialized in the name of my favourite building on Jalan Ampang, the euphonious but totally undistinguished Wisma Selangor Dredging. Kuala Lumpur was becoming a prosperous place. And it was not surprising that it became the capital of the newly Federated Malay States which combined Selangor, Negri Sembilan, Perak and Pahang. The reservoir at Ampang provided piped water for a population of around 25,000. New buildings began to emerge. The State Sec-retariat (later named Sultan Abdul Samad Building and now the site of Judicial Department and High Courts), built in 1894, was one of the first government projects to be completed. The cen-tral tower of the ornate building, which fuses Victorian architec-ture with Mogul overtones, houses Kuala Lumpur's version of Big Ben: the clock was installed during Queen Victoria's birthday celebrations in 1897. The local scuttlebutt at the time concerned

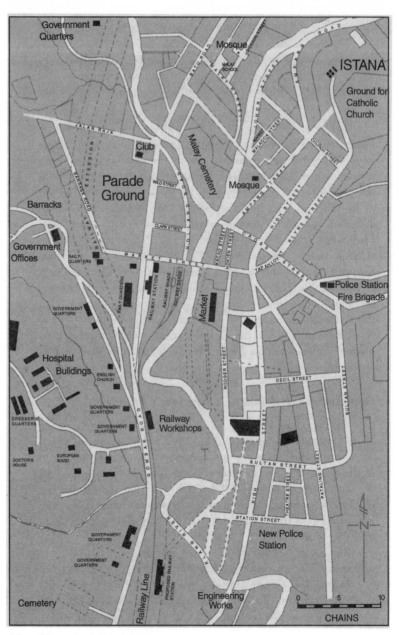

Map of the centre of Kuala Lumpur, 1889.

the fear that this tower was in imminent threat of collapse; today the local wags have very similar thoughts about the new Petronas Twin Towers, the tallest building in the world.

At the turn of the century, a new cash crop made its first appearance in the Klang valley. Selangor coffee plantations had been declining for some decades, helped along with disease, poor yields and a drop in coffee prices. It was a demanding crop that required some shade from the scorching tropical sun. Legend has it that between the coffee bushes, a tree called *Hevea brasiliensis* was planted, to provide shade. The tree was promoted by H. N. Ridley, locally known as Mad Ridley, director of the Singapore Botanic Gardens. Ridley had a habit of surreptitiously slipping seeds into the jackets of coffee planters, knowing that they would be thrown out upon discovery and would grow wherever they were thrown. He came to be known as the father of the Malayan rubber industry, for the trees he encouraged were rubber trees. The emergence of the car, and the manufacture of tyres, meant that the demand for rubber soared; by 1905, rubber had become one of the major export crops of Malaysia.

The Chinese labourers proved to be insufficient to man the newly developed rubber estates. So Indian labourers were imported in large numbers to service the expanding rubber industry. The majority of the Indian immigrants were Tamil Hindus from South India, but Sikhs and Punjabi Muslims (sometimes mistakenly called 'Pathans') from North India also arrived in significant numbers. Most of the Tamil immigrants worked in the rubber estates, while the Sikhs tended to find work as watchmen or policemen. A few families added to the traditional community of Chettiers, moneylenders, foreign exchange brokers as we would call them today and indeed as they are now employed in the money changing booths scattered all over town. They became an important and influential South Indian group. One of the most famous figures in the Indian community was Thambusamy Pillai, who came to Selangor in 1875 as a clerk in the Resident's office at Klang. However, he soon moved into moneylending, tin mining and contractual work for the imperial government, becoming rich

71

in a rather short time. He is said to have known everybody who was anybody and was, in turn, known and admired by many: people queued to be invited for a memorable hot curry in his house. Passionate about racing, Pillai was a prominent member of the Selangor Club. But he is remembered mostly for his ability to build bridges and for his legacy to his community: the famous Sri Maha Mariamman Temple on Jalan Bandar, a boundary of today's Chinatown, and just across the road from a Chinese temple. The highly ornate Hindu temple typical of South Indian religious architecture was built in 1873.

While the natives and immigrants worked, the Europeans played. Champagne and crabs, cricket and clubs were the order of the day. The Selangor Club was the first popular place for the Europeans to gather. It is located and still stands out in its mock Tudor black-and-white distinctiveness, directly opposite the imposing administrative building named after Sultan Ahmad Samad. Between the two was the *padang*, the playing fields, now known as Merdeka Square. Until very recently one could still watch cricket being played here, which is exactly what happened the moment I time-warped into my first visit. My love for cricket notwithstanding, the Edwardianness of it all was almost too much for me. The club, in certain circles, is known as the 'Spotted Dog' and there are a number of stories relating how it acquired its unusual name. One tells of the police commissioner's wife, a frequent visitor, who use to tie her two Dalmatians outside the club while she sipped gin and tonic inside. But the most probable reason for the name was the club's practice of accepting a few locals as members. The dispensation was used more by Indians than Malays or Chinese who were, at the time, less impressed by club life. In 1890, the Lake Club, which still stands and is still a club, was formed for Europeans who did not want to mix with Asians. Taking its name from its location in Lake Gardens, the luscious 70-hectare park, it had very high subscription fees designed to keep out even the less well-heeled tommies. The imperial lifestyle is still emulated, after a fashion, in these clubs.

VIII

One could read most of the history of Kuala Lumpur from my balcony in Menarah Indahh. It was written all over the buildings and dwellings one could see on a clear day. The tallest flagpole in the world, shooting up from the ground in Merdeka Square, faintly visible from my bedroom window, speaks volumes of Malaysia's struggle for independence. The strange Tabang Hajji building, a concave tower with 'Allah', in familiar Arabic calligraphy, pasted on the top, declared the long history of Islamic presence in the region. The artificial lake that was the Ampang tin quarry was a mine of information, not least because of numerous legends associated with it, on the political economy of the region. The minarets, the towers of temples (both Hindu and Buddhist), conveyed the multicultural past of the city. Even the words and descriptions one hears are pregnant with meaning. The expatriate inhabitants of Menarah Indahh are collectively known by the common local designation, *mat salleh*, an indigenous comment on colonial history. It is derived from 'mad sailors' who came to the peninsula in search of colonies and went crazy in the ports and elsewhere. The Chinese simply call them *kwai lo*: foreign devils. Every construction, simple or ornate, humble or ostentatious, that I observe from my balcony has real history and real myth associated with it. The city whispered constantly, narrating tales of people and ghosts, real and imaginary, jungle campaigns and adventures, legendary and not so legendary – for all those who could hear.

But then the skyline of Kuala Lumpur began to change irredeemably. Every so often, I saw a new building emerge from nowhere, block out my view and obliterate history. It was as though someone had bought a job lot of discarded Western designs and was building them all simultaneously and at an accelerated pace. One morning, I got up reasonably early and, as usual, went straight to the balcony and opened the doors. I paid no attention to the giant crane that had appeared overnight because

Laila and Majnun did not fly out as was their custom. I looked for them on the wall where they normally slept – they were not there. I scanned the entire ceiling, carefully scrutinized the walls, but could not find them. Then I heard wings flapping. Guided by the sound I found them on the floor next to an old planter's chair. Laila was dead: one of her wings and the lower part of her body had been eaten. Majnun was flapping next to her. He seemed to fly straight into the wall, crash down, pick himself up again, and hit the wall. I picked him up and placed him on the palm of my hand. He stayed there motionless for a few seconds, then flapped again and became totally inert.

I knew Kuala Lumpur would never be the same again.

The Circumference of the Mall

Kuala Lumpur began as a shop. On the banks of a river, connected and connecting, the city began as a shop. And people
came from all parts of the East and then the West. I retrace an
ancient cycle as I find the city for the first time. My primal
image of this city is its primal essence, for my experience of
Kuala Lumpur began with the Mall. Malling, as I named the act
of wandering aimlessly around the innumerable shopping centres that sprout up everywhere like secondary jungle undergrowth, has taught me and opened my eyes to much of what I
know about the city. Kuala Lumpur began as a late expression
of the history that formed it. For much of its own history, as we
saw in chapter 1, Kuala Lumpur was off-centre to the developments that eventually made it a capital city. Fittingly, the city is
itself off-centre, or has no single central area, but at least three
distinct hubs around which cluster numerous residential areas.
Malays insist, quite properly, that to understand Malay culture
and Malaysian society you have to grasp the character of the
kampung. Only with time and experience do you come to understand that Kuala Lumpur is itself a distillation of *kampung*, a
great gathering that has no meaning without the innumerable
villages from which its citizens originate; the whole nation is
now the hinterland of this city. And as it is the principal gathering place of the nation nothing about Malaysia can be compre-
hended without the influence that radiates out from Kuala
Lumpur, the gathering place of all power where all deals and
decisions are made. Connected and connecting KL describes all
the cycles and circles enfolding the past, the present and the
future. There are *kampung* right inside the city, behind or around
the corner from each of the central districts where the shopping

malls mushroom overnight. Malling around the shops, ancient, modern and postmodern, you get to know a city, its history and the history it makes. In a city and a country formed by trading connections, shopping is the connective tissue, the lifeblood and essential ingredient that makes all apparent and comprehensible.

I made my way by taxi from the airport. This was the old Lapan Terbang Antarabangsa Subang, the friendly, homely old airport that was *continua*lly morphing to accommodate upwardly mobile travelling tastes before being abandoned in favour of the newly made 'airport in the jungle', the largest in Southeast Asia. At the new Sepang Airport you can observe jungle encased in glass like a pickled specimen. When I first arrived at the old airport, you drove along a highway cut through rubber and oil palm plantations and felt you were within the jungle itself. This was before they put up the signs assuring people that such commercial undertakings greened the earth, and then had to quickly take them down again as the estates were sold to developers to make way for urban sprawl.

We continued on through the industrial sprawl of PJ, Petaling Jaya, the first satellite of KL. PJ is a deeply perplexing, impenetrable annexe to the city, a mixture of factories and residential areas, where the unwary get lost in a complex layout of streets that have no apparent logic. Seemingly it just grew, exuberantly and randomly, a true urban jungle. I have been that jungle explorer whose sense of direction is befuddled by the branching roadways and paths only to emerge hours later thoroughly lost, exhausted and confused, only one junction from where I first began and no nearer to finding my destination. Residents of KL fear the complexities of PJ and city taxi drivers often decline to carry you there lest they too get lost in the urban jungle. When I went to live for a time in PJ, I soon went native and learned to relish the illogical diversionary tactics that keep its byways for local use only.

Leaving PJ we pass the yet-to-be yuppified hills of Bangsar where just one condo, from a distance resembling the forbidding style of East European public housing and known locally as the Berlin Wall, stood out on the hilltop, a harbinger of things to come. We then hit another stretch of highway divided and lined with resplendently manicured plants and shrubbery and overlooked by trees. It seemed we had diverged from the city back into the countryside. It is one of the delights of KL that, starting almost anywhere, you take a turning in the road and seem to have entered the countryside or wandered into a garden. But this imposing stretch of highway leads to the ultramodern parliament building, the Dewan Rayat, the spiked roof of which peaks over the treetops. We sweep on until we come to a new, more open vista of brand-new skyscrapers surrounding a large modern building designed in honour of a traditional Malay house. This, appropriately enough, is the Putra World Trade Centre. I recall Tomas Pires's comments on Malacca, the emporium of all the world. Here in the modern capital is a planned and developed world emporium suffixed by the soil, *putra*, the land, the whole nation geared to trading, as it ever was. Nestled behind is the Pan Pacific Hotel, where I was to stay.

I was amongst the first guests of the Pan Pac – in KL every name is shortened – and have a natural, or perhaps an unnatural, affinity for the hotel. During the 1980s I stayed there regularly and have patronized its restaurants as a natural part of my excursions around the city thereafter. Over the course of our acquaintance I have noted how the Pan Pac has reflected the changes in Kuala Lumpur itself. A modern building, a perpendicular tower of concrete and glass: the window of each of its rooms takes up an entire wall and is encased with decorative cement work in deference to what is glibly called Islamic architecture. For all that the building was big and imposing, in the days of our first meeting, it had a human and humble quality to it. The lobby was open to the outside world and was thus flooded with natural light. It had a perspective, an outlook. Wherever you walked or sat in the circular confines of the lobby you had a context: you could see what was going on across the road; or watch the River Gombak winding its way to the 'muddy junction'; or simply observe the passing traffic in all the shades and varieties of Malaysia's cultures. The hotel, like the city, was at ease with itself.

Then, the Pan Pacific began to be postmodernized. The lobby was rebuilt so that now it is totally closed to the outside world. It has no perspective. You could be looking anywhere and you would be looking nowhere. It is dark and claustrophobic in its tiled and wood-panelled elegance. The hotel itself has become faceless and inhuman – once inside, you could be in any hotel, anywhere in the world. And where once everyone knew you by your first name, now no one sees you, let alone knows you. A fake culture has taken over, exemplified most notably by the nightly entertainment in the 'Lobby Lounge' where visiting pop groups from the Philippines play chart toppers whose lyrics have been learned phonetically to bizarre effect. But nothing is as bizarre inside the Pan Pacific as can be found outside it: right opposite the hotel is the Mall, the first postmodern institution to grace the city.

II

The building of the Mall marked a decisive moment in Kuala Lumpur's history: it is at this juncture that Kuala Lumpur set its sights on leap-frogging into postmodern times, almost before postmodernism had been invented. Although the Mall was not the first shopping complex to be built in Kuala Lumpur, and there is now an overabundance of 'one-stop shopping, enter-tainment and dining centres', the Mall does have the distinction of being the first truly postmodern structure in Kuala Lumpur. It is a place where different worlds, histories, traditions and art forms are collapsed, homogenized, commodified and sold. Its wave-like roof cocooned shoppers in an attempt to focus their attention away from the fountain and the lights to Yohan, the Japanese superstore, on one side, and branded shops positively screaming with the latest fashions and accessories on the other.

The Mall after a series of expansions.

The first floor, replete with more shops, also hosts traditional stalls where Malay women sell jewellery and handicrafts. The top floor has two halves: on one side, Malaysia's largest indoor amusement park, the 'Starlight Express'; on the other, a replica of the historical city of Malacca. The postmodern pastiche of faux-façade shop-fronts and houses enfolds, refers to and contains real history, real connections. Under a postmodern roof you can wander along 'Medan Hang Tuah', 'Melaka Street', 'Penang Street' and 'Love Lane'. After experiencing the Tornado roller coasters, dodgem cars, the Matterhorn and the swinging Spanish ship, one could take a walk straight into fabricated history, enveloped in the rich smells of local foods. For behind the ersatz shop-fronts selling handicrafts there is a food court, as such places have come to be called, with postmodern yet authentic hawker stalls.

In its first phase of expansion, the Mall acquired the Cathay Cineplex, which shows Hollywood films and Hong Kong fare, as well as a host of new shops. Over the years I've known it, the Mall, like Kuala Lumpur, has been undergoing continual rebuilding and expansion. Subsequent expansions transformed the

79

The primal essence of Kuala Lumpur: 'shopping centres that sprout up everywhere like secondary jungle undergrowth'.

shopping centre into an entire city complex with the addition of a great tower of offices, another great tower housing the Legend Hotel and a network of condominiums, modern perpendicular tower blocks crossed with a rationalized Mediterranean flavour. Then Yohan became impoverished and transformed into 'Aktif Lifestyles Stores, formerly known as Yohan'.

At the Mall, multicultural eclecticism rules, by a strict seasonal rotation of fair shares for all. In a country that has no seasons, festivals mark the passage of the year, often inspired by other people's seasons. I used to think that the best guarantee of perpetual employment would be to embrace a career as a shopping centre decorative display designer. One would move seamlessly from working on Christmas to Chinese New Year, Valentine's Day, Easter, Mother's Day, Father's Day, Deepavali, the Hindu festival of lights, and of course Hari Raya, literally the resplendent day. There are two Hari Raya; the one that marks the end of the Muslim fasting month of Ramadan is the main Malay celebration of the year. There are additional high days and holidays and marketing scams liberally sprinkled throughout the course of each year. For each occasion buildings and especially shops are decorated, and the Mall makes a fetish of being elaborate and effusive in bedecking itself for each festival. The waterfall would disappear, overnight, and a stage would emerge to take up a large part of the foyer. The stage could be elaborately decorated, with a traditional *kampung* scene, a spring day in rural China or a Hansel and Gretel gingerbread house covered in snow. It could host musical acts, dances or marketing competitions that draw huge impassable crowds. You do not go to the Mall to pick up a few necessities and leave; you visit the Mall for a fully marketed lifestyle experience.

My very first acquaintance with the Mall spanned the time when it was preparing for Christmas; indeed all of KL was getting ready. One staggered into the Mall to escape the glaring sun, 92 °F heat, with a similar level of humidity, to be encased in hyperactive air-conditioning. So cold was the environment within that polystyrene snowflakes were forming at every conceivable point and dripping down in flurries from the ceiling. The gingerbread house on the stage acquired a new layer of cotton wool snow everyday. Thus prepared, you entered a shop to be bombarded by dreams of a white Christmas blaring from concealed loudspeakers. Wandering on, through further snowdrifts that cut you off from the outside world, under arches of tinsel surrounded by spruce trees (artificial) bedecked with dark red ribbons and sparkling silver and golden balls, you begin to believe the dream. I would repeat this disorienting excursion every day as a daily constitutional, or deconditioning exercise, a trip into genuine postmodern confusion. But the influence, I soon detected, was pervasive. In the lobby of the Pan Pac, where I was staying, a sleigh and Santa's reindeer made their appearance beside an elaborately dressed Christmas tree, just waiting for the man himself to put in an appearance. You could order a special fruit punch drink served in a ceramic Santa-shaped container, and for a small extra sum take the Santa home with you. Forget the tin mines, my friends and I concluded; somewhere in this country there must be cotton wool mines where exploited elves were working overtime to meet the ever-increasing demand for make-believe snow. Then the coffee shop began to undergo major renovation. A huge plasterboard brick structure was installed – for what? To represent an open fireplace, just what one would need in KL's climate! Another hotel went so far as to have an actual, live flame gas fire in their plasterboard grate, which seemed to me far too literal to be acceptably postmodern, nothing so much as decidedly daft. We went there merely to laugh. Whereas you had to walk out of the Mall and stand stock still for a few minutes of reacclimatization, taking in the palm trees, the sun, the heat, by way of a reality check.

I go to the Mall to buy a specific product. On the first floor, buried inside a record store, is the shop of my friend Jimmy. It is very easy to miss him: the loud audio and visual output of the record shop does not allow anyone to focus on anything, pick out the detail and perceive that there is a shop within a shop. Behind the façade of the real economy, there is another economy.

One manifestation of postmodernism in Kuala Lumpur is the strong political economy of the fake. If there is no difference between the real and the imaginary, the object and its image, as postmodernism maintains, than the real is as good as the fake. And the fakes that one finds in KL, and the region in general, are not just any fakes – they are genuine fakes. It is not marketing hype. Digital music sounds exactly the same whether it is on a real CD – that is, the one sold by its manufacturer – or on a fake CD, the copied version sold everywhere by street vendors and hawkers. This underground economy has played an important, although unrecognized, part in the development of Kuala Lumpur. Jimmy sells fake films.

Even though his shop cannot be seen easily, Jimmy can spot his potential customers the instant they appear on his floor. He will cleverly manoeuvre you into his secret enclave – all the time dropping the names of the latest Hollywood blockbusters. Jimmy sells three distinct varieties of fakes and an experienced customer will insist on knowing the pedigree of the imitation. The commonest type is the film that has actually been refilmed. This involves smuggling a Super-8 video camera inside a cinema and recording the proceedings. Invariably, the sound quality of the copies tends to be bad. Often you get only part of the film. It is not that the entire performance has not been recorded, just that the secret recorder got a seat too near and a bit off-centre of the big screen, so physics being physics, not all the action fits into the lens of his Super-8. But this is compensated by an added value: the postmodern experience of observing the observers, witnessing audience reactions and enjoyment – or not – of the film. One can hear the audience laughing, booing, hissing and gasping with fear or excitement as well as witness their excursions to buy popcorn or visits to the toilet. The added value is invaluable material for the truly critical viewer.

The next sort is the film that is not quite yet a film. This is what one would imagine to be the final, pre-release director's cut and it comes complete with time codes at the bottom of the screen. The visual and sound quality of these copies is rather good but that is not their main strength. They have an extra postmodern dimension that the real video does not contain. The ending in these 'fake films' can sometimes be different from the commercially released version, or contain scenes that do not make it to the cinema. There is a logical explanation to this mystery. Initial audience previews, before a film is released, sometimes cause the director or the studio to change the ending or trim the running time. This, of course, is not only an invaluable asset for students of film but also an economic boon for Jimmy. Sometimes, he sells his pre-release fake with one ending and cheap at the price together with the released version at inflated market prices. The world of fakes is a win–win world.

The last type of fake film in Jimmy's lair is the film that is more than a film. This variety is copied on video from a laser disc, so here we have digitized picture and sound. The video comes in two parts, divided by several minutes of blank screen – this is where the laser discs are being changed. This is not the only change involved. In pirate videos the sound is always recorded in reverse – the main channel carries the music and sound effects and the dialogue is demoted to the secondary channel. This is not surprising really, since the Southeast Asian audiences are, on the whole, more interested in bang, bang, wham than banter, banter, silence. So the film jumps out of the screen every time a gun is fired, a car crashes or a punch is thrown – and then fades back into background noise that can just about be distinguished as dialogue. There are added dimensions to the picture as well. It could slow down, freeze up, speed up or burst into billions of pixels and then morph into its original digital form. All this means the laser disc copies invariably tend to be longer than the original films. So you get, as Jimmy says, more for your less money.

Now Jimmy is not just any merchant: he is a philosopher-merchant, a Chinese businessmen who is also intensely Malaysian. Buying from Jimmy is not a transaction; it is a social relationship. A real film buff, Jimmy is much more than a *Halliwell's* on two feet. The famed Bible of the film world only

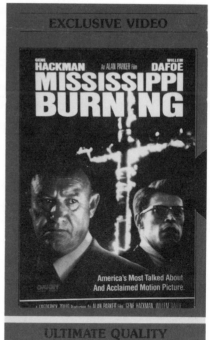

Spot the fake!

covers the films of Hollywood. Jimmy can talk with equal facility about American, Hong Kong, Taiwanese, Indian, Indonesian
and Malaysian cinema. He introduced me to the films of the
Hong Kong director John Wu, and action actor, Chow Yun-Fat,
long before they became cult figures in the West. Both, Jimmy
predicted, would migrate to Hollywood and lose their poetic
edge. He has proved right on both accounts. Jimmy's philosophy is rather simple: he is a die-hard believer in free speech and
free trade. And you get plenty of both at his shop. His regular
customers are showered with a generous dose of abuse directed
at the ignorantly applied prurience of the local censors, drowned
in reportage of the local political scene and how it is destroying
the indigenous film and media industry, and drenched with liberal references to Malay proverbs. There is one that Jimmy cites
more than frequently: 'one should never interfere with another
man's rice bowl'. When he has repeated this proverb more than

85

once in less than ten minutes, you know the counterfeit police have been around. But Jimmy takes these raids in his stride. He is constantly under threat of being closed down, run out of business or having his contraband confiscated. But the threat is as fake, or indeed real, as the films he sells. Jimmy is scrupulously honest and more than generous to his regular customers. If he thinks it is a bad film and if he knows the copy to be poor, he will sell you a film only reluctantly and then only if you insist. So buying a film from Jimmy is not a simple affair – the ritual involves three distinct steps. First, you ask if he has the film that will be released in New York in a couple of weeks. 'Got, got', he will reply enthusiastically and then launch into a colourful critique quoting advance reviews and gossip he has acquired over the Internet, before giving his own verdict: 'story no good, *lah*'. Jimmy likes films with strong narratives, meandering, cyclic plots that, in the final analysis, like *Sejarah Malayu*, have something to say. It is not surprising, then, that he dislikes most of the films he actually sells. So we move to the second part of the process. Does he actually have a decent copy of this film with a rotten story? 'Copy no good, *lah*! Two weeks, two weeks. Good copy in two weeks.' If you insist he will actually slip the film in the video set up at the corner of his shop and let you decide for yourself. We thus move to the final phase. Can I have a lousy copy of this lousy film, please? It is at this point that Jimmy disappears. He grabs a carrier bag and runs out of the shop at great speed. Ten, fifteen, twenty minutes later he reappears triumphantly holding a reasonably watchable copy – invariably with added value. 'Bring it back if you don't like it!', he says, as he slips the naked video into a flashy, shrink-wrapped cover. He means it. When I don't like a film, when the yarn is not to my taste, I take it back and Jimmy exchanges it for a film that I think I would like.

Like Jimmy's added-value films, there is more to this business than meets the eye. The world of fake goods is not limited to music and films. All manner of designer products – from watches, sunglasses to clothes and shoes, as well as computer

A postcard view of Chinatown, Kuala Lumpur.

software, spare parts for cars and machinery – are available as
real fakes. The Mall, where Jimmy carries on his enterprise,
looks and feels like a place of genuine imitation. But genuine
imitation is actually the guarantee loudly proclaimed by the
stall-holders of Petaling Street, in the heart of KL's Chinatown,
a place that positively reeks of history, thanks mostly to the
oldest drains in the city. 'Come, look, genuine imitation, real
fakes!', the smiling young purveyors of fake watches cry as they
lure tourists to their stalls. Petaling Street is a traditional thoroughfare lined with Chinese shop-houses, selling all variety of
merchandise, the covered pavements and mouths of alleyways
host hawker food stalls, around which cluster tables and chairs
for the diners. Negotiating your way along Petaling Street
would be a sufficient obstacle course without the addition of
what brings everyone here, the real front of the fake economy.
For the street is double-parked with market stalls. To visit the
stalls you must walk in the roadway as traffic snakes and snarls

and jostles among the shoppers. Around 6 p.m. everyday the cars are banished and Petaling Street becomes the most famous and populous night market in KL. Two more lines of edge-to-edge stalls are set up in the middle of the road and crowds of shoppers negotiate their way from stall to stall in an enclosed, heaving and sweaty mass. As well as the real imitations, there are stalls selling fruit, stalls selling sweets – at least that is how they appear to the casual observer; on examination they turn out to be things such as sour plums that are both salty and sour with a background of sweetness. There are stalls selling refreshing drinks: sea coconut and cat's eye juice (it's a fruit) at one end of the street and at the other a real sugar cane juice outfit. This delectable juice requires peeled trimmed lengths of raw sugar cane. The sticks are fed through a contraption that looks and operates exactly like an old-fashioned mangle, the kind people used to use to wring out their washing. From one part of the device comes the pulp of the mangled sticks and from another the green and delicious juice, the best thirst-quencher known to man. Petaling Street looks, feels, tastes and smells like another world. It is old Asia, populous and alive, a part of the old Indian Ocean world, one with the spirit of that world that kept on trying to subvert and reorganize around the fringes of the colonial order and the growth of industrial modernity, from which it was excluded. Petaling Street continues the resistance.

Southeast and East Asia are where cheap electronics and the high-tech ingredients of all information technology as well as much else are manufactured in bulk. It is also counterfeit country. There is no contradiction here. Those who labour in the factories to produce all the consumer desirables often earn too little to buy the genuine branded end products, which, despite local component production, end up as costly imports from other countries. In KL low-income groups need never suffer from the true definition of poverty, which is not absolute absence of disposable income, but the socially more cutting and cruel fate of not being able to participate in the consumerist illusions of the postmodern era. The fake economy, the inability to tell the real from the imitation, enables those with little money to keep themselves in the game of social presentation and fashion permutations. Slight Malay bodies clad in fake designer jeans, fake T-shirts, wrists adorned with fake designer watches, clutching fake designer bags and cloned mobile phones look as if they have wandered straight out of Beverly Hills for the pittance the get-up cost them. They are *in*-cluded, fashion and fancy, and not *ex*-cluded, marginalized onlookers. In the international politics of self and style they are fully empowered. And the transformation can be accomplished within the ambience and precincts of living history.

Kuala Lumpur is not unlike Jimmy's different categories of videos, underpinned by the spirit of Petaling Street. Development, after all, is fundamentally, philosophically, entirely about imitation. Kuala Lumpur strategizes genuine imitation for itself and the whole nation. It looks to the glamour and glitter not merely of Hollywood but also of Japan, Korea, Taiwan and Singapore. Development, as many have learned, can be a real fake. So genuine imitation requires that the provenance of the process be scrutinized with a practised eye. The economy of genuine imitation requires skills, artifice and considerable acumen both ancient indigenous and modern imported. Old skills and facilities are essential to making the process possible and what is possible is to appear and in many senses to be part of a new order, a postmodern reordering of global realities. KL has a foothold in all the stages, expressions and appearances of each and every stage from the old Indian Ocean dynamic to the forefront of the future of globalized cyberspace. In many instances its stories have or seek different endings from the branded product, and one can prefer an alternative scenario. Genuine imitation is also subtle subversion allowing authentic local ideas and imperatives to be included and empowered in ways not designed for, intended for or even to the taste of audiences elsewhere. Kuala Lumpur is involved in many ways, on many levels in the international politics of style and self. It achieves its sense of place through enterprise and artifice that retains, employs and works through institutions, organizations and ideas that are distinctively its own and not beholden to anyone else's patternbook. And sometimes its labours are just a fraud.

Chinatown holds many other attractions besides Petaling Street. There are the noxious fumes of the dried fish shops, the porcelain purveyors who swell with pride when they tell you the bowls and vases they sell are 'China made!' – self-evident guarantee of quality! There are the old-fashioned higgledy-piggledy shops that sell odds and ends of everything. These are the kind of places you visit to match one lost button from a favourite garment or to find an exotic wing nut to repair a beloved machine. And they sell them one by one, for a few *sens* (pennies) – not as job lots encased in layers of packaging, insisting you must have six when you have no earthly use for more than one. There is the alley of the flower sellers, Orchid Lane as I call it. Here they sell the peculiar floral arrangements essential for all formal special occasions and grand openings; they look like funeral wreaths mounted on easels. But the most intriguing shops are those selling Chinese religious necessaries. Necessary for what I am not sure, but there are bright red altar niches for hanging at appropriate places or just set down by the roadside. Incense that comes in all shapes and sizes up to and including great beehive-shaped spirals a few feet high and inches thick that hang outside Chinese temples. There are jars of scented oils and all manner of red and gold decorations and lion masks and sundry other curious objects that stimulate the imagination as you wander in and just gaze around. Moving in a proper Chinese shop is never advisable; there is always too much merchandise stacked everywhere leaving only the narrowest and most precarious space for ingress and egress. They always remind me of the famous passage in Foucault's *The Order of Things*, the place where he quotes Borges's reflection on an ancient Chinese list of categories. So different is the set of categories, its tally of this next to that, from European expectations that both authors use the example to reflect on the impossibility of thinking that way. It is safer to stand still and just look!

Chinatown, and within it Petaling Street, exude the ambience of an older world flavoured with juxtaposition and contradiction that befits the original hub from which KL emerged. Just down the road, on the banks of the river, is the Central Market; it used to be the city's wet market and must be in almost the exact place where the first shop was built. Today, the Central Market houses handicraft shopping that reflects this crossroads of Asia and is an ideal place to see the works of local artists. You can buy any amount of Thai or Indonesian goodies. You could get yourself a Chinese name seal, a blank stone on the bottom of which your name can be carved in Chinese characters. Or you could go for some of the traditional Malay crafts that have not been totally downgraded thanks to the influence and ethos of the Ministry of Tourism. You could buy a piece of *songket*, a heavy cloth interwoven with gold thread, which is an integral part of the modern traditional costume of Malay men. Or you could watch batik silk scarves being hand-painted by young Malay ladies before your eyes, just next to the table where an ancient Chinese artist, in the sense of a very old gentleman, flicks out paintings of koi carp in traditional brush-stroke style. There is a booth where you and a companion can dress and have your photograph taken as a proper Malay bridal couple. You could buy a *wau*, the wonderful Malay kite, or pick up a *chongkat*, a carved boat-like object with two rows of receptacles along the top for playing a Malay game something akin to backgammon. The tourist 'must haves' include the shop dedicated to Royal Selangor Pewter. The Royal is a relatively new addition, but pewter, an alloy made largely from tin, is an old indigenous product morphed into a new industry. Little decorative plaques of pewter are an inescapable acquisition of living in KL. They are always presented as gifts to participants in any formal conference or function, and life in KL moves to the rhythm of conscientious conferring. Much as I appreciate Selangor Pewter, royally indeed, over the years I have come to appreciate concomitantly the Malaysian etiquette of gift giving. Gifts are received richly encased in decorative wrapping; you accept them with thanks and delight and immediately set them aside unopened. This is to ensure there is never a 'loss of face' for the giver should you dislike the item. It's not that I dislike engraved pewter plaques; it is just a matter of having limited use and space for the inordinate number it is possible to acquire in a very limited amount of residence and business in KL. The day the custom switches to handing out the lovely, and always useful, pewter picture frames is the day I return to the conference circuit. Pewter plaques are for ordinary mortals. At the Central Market shop of my friend Rohanna you can see the encased specimens of Kelantan silver work, objects presented to really important people: an elaborately worked silver *kris*, an ashtray in the form of a *rembana*, the enormous traditional kettle drum or a traditional Malay house crafted in silver.

Before they started encasing the whole area under concrete pylons to support the elevated light railway, you could take a delightful walk along the riverbank. Starting from the Central Market, you ambled along a pathway lined with frangipani trees, until you met the road-bridge. From the bridge you could

The Market, Kuala Lumpur, *c.* 1884.

92

Jalan Tungku Abdul Rahman is still the home of local shopping but now hosts wall-to-wall cars as well.

see the Mesjid Jamek, the beautiful little mosque whose Mughal-style cupolas and arches encase a cool, open prayer hall. It sits on the point of land where the two rivers, the Klang and the Gombak, meet and nestle among palm trees while being over-looked by huge high-rise modern skyscrapers. Turn left over the road-bridge and in moments you are on the old *padang*, now Dataran Merdeka, Independence Square. This is the colonial heart of KL. The two long sides of the rectangular square are formed by Sultan Abdul Samad Building, now the Law Courts and across the green centre the mock-Tudor Selangor Club. The short end of the square is completed by the little Anglican Cathedral, and nearby stands the Clock Tower, just at the entrance to Jalan Tunku Abdul Rahman. Another night market occupies this busy street every Saturday night. I am always struck by the incongruity of the silversmith's shop, just as you leave the square and enter Jalan Tunku Abdul Rahman. The shop looks as if it had lost its bearings and fetched up here direct from Old Holborn. I visualize Edwardian sportsmen staggering over from the Selangor Club ordering up cups and medals for their

93

competitions. The rest of the street is local shopping territory, a long stretch of colonnaded shop fronts intercut with dark arcades occupied entirely by sellers of batik silk. At amazing bargain prices you can buy washable silk in four-and-a-half metre pieces, ready-printed or hand-painted, to be made up into the ubiquitous Malay ladies' outfit, the *baju kurung*. Jalan Tunku Abdul Rahman is the hub of textile shopping in Kuala Lumpur, in all cultural varieties. Take a large breath – there's no air available within – and plunge through one of the arcades and you will emerge on Jalan Masjid India, KL's little India, where shops selling all manner of Indian goods and textiles mingle with Indian restaurants and Chettier money changers.

It takes two hours to negotiate, in all senses, the half-mile of Petaling Street. In Petaling Street haggling over price, purchasing as performance art – the better the performance the better the price – is the order of the day and night. By the end of this time one needs not refreshment but sustenance. Every kind of food at every imaginable type of eatery is available in KL. On Jalan Tunku Abdul Rahman is the old colonial eatery, the Coliseum, where sizzling steak is still served up in an ambience of perpetually fading grandeur. Wherever you look in the city there is an outlet for any and every variant of franchised fast food known to modern merchandising. There are elegant watering holes of the new Asian cuisine, like the delightful Bon Ton, in an old house lovingly maintained. When I first knew it, it used to be an antique shop-cum-restaurant. Now it's exclusively fine wining and dining, and be sure to leave enough space for their stupendous puddings and cakes – housed and displayed in an enormous refrigerator. But Petaling Street always puts me in the mood for genuine hawker food and that means a trip to Bangsar. If Petaling Street is the most famous night market, then Bangsar used to be the most famous all-night congress of hawker stalls.

A hawker stall is an essential feature of the KL scene. It is a complicated, wonderful piece of ingenuity. The original form lurked on pavements and street corners and was an elaborate barrow with its own awning, complete with food storage and display space as well as mobile cooking facilities where traders, the hawkers, prepare local delicacies, Malay, Chinese or Indian, on the spot, freshly made for modest sums. Tables and chairs will cluster under a tentative marquee, a large sheet of plastic suspended aloft to protect diners from the rain and glare of the sun. It is usually clean, the stall that is, for the environs tend to get bestrewn with rubbish and rather foetid in short order, adding to without detracting from the experience; almost always safe to eat at, even for delicate tourist constitutions. And when you find the right stall, the right hawker, since each specializes in a limited repertoire of dishes, you can experience a culinary masterpiece. You can sit at the roadside surrounded by the detritus of cooking and the fumes of passing traffic and eat like a king. In a postmodern locale such as the Mall the entire concept has been fixed, updated and upgraded into a 'food court', where only the food remains the same. But in Bangsar each night the original variety of stalls would expand from the pavements, where a few operated during the day, and take over an entire street. You could weave your way from stall to stall as diners sit at the tables and chairs set out in the roadway and consider which delicacy fits your mood. There are, however, other sophisticated considerations. A plethora of hawker stalls is a multicultural minefield. Malays do not eat at Chinese stalls where pork may have been prepared, Indians seek out Indian stalls where no beef is on offer or only vegetarian fare is prepared. But anyone and everyone can find some Chinese, Malay or Indian stalls that prepare some suitable and safe local dish.

Bangsar and Damansara are another hub of the off-centre city. I used to work in Bangsar at the old TV3 offices tucked away behind the *New Straits Times* complex, where a number of local newspapers are printed. These back streets were lined with hawker stalls that operated as the office canteen. Not that the TV3 and the *Straits Times* did not have in-house canteens. When you meet people in KL they will ask politely how you are, then they will get really concerned for your wellbeing:

'Have you taken your lunch?', they will inquire, which in Malay is resolved to the basic form of 'Have you eaten rice?' Sustenance is all, and the more sustenance available the better. Modern air-conditioned buildings are an assault on tropical dispositions. The air-conditioning is always turned up to the freeze-drying setting. So a short trip out into the air, to see the sun and avert incipient frostbite, keeps your bodily functions in order. TV3's building was particularly arctic, so not surprisingly the favourite stall out in the street specialized in dishes richly laden with *prit*, the tiny neutron bomb of the chilli family, which counterbalanced the air-conditioning with internal thermal insulation. Food should be taken in small bursts at regular intervals during the day, allowing for numerous trips into the warm blanket of the open air. In KL the air is a tactile, enveloping, physical presence: moist, hot and nurturing, especially after air-conditioned buildings. Since everyone spends long hours at the office and often commutes long distances to and from work, the sustenance intervals are a proper, legitimate, accepted part of the work routine. At a definite moment each afternoon the Malay news manager at TV3 would raise his head from his grindstone and declare with determination 'tosai!' This was a general summons for all who could tear themselves away from their own grindstones to join him on an excursion. At *tosai* time the stalls outside the building just would not suffice. We would make our way up the hill to the main thoroughfare of Bangsar stalls to a particular Tamil hawker who served delicious *dhosas*, the thin fermented rice pancakes served with curry dip and vegetable accoutrements, which in local parlance are called *tosai*. As we prepared to return to the office the street would be getting ready for its nightly transformation into the premiere hub of local night dining.

New office blocks rise around the city and they all have multiple fast food outlets incorporated within their fabric. But no sooner are they occupied than they acquire an encrustation of genuine hawker stalls on any bit of waste ground around the perimeter or even on the pavements outside. You can take a

Redeveloped Bangsar, the latest in new-wave shopping centres.

Malaysian into the postmodern era, but their stomachs provide a rooted reality check. What, I often wonder, do Malaysians need with Americanized fast food when they have their own varieties? *Nasi lemak*, for example, is aboriginal fast food provided by traditional hawker enterprise and all biodegradable. It is a feast of rice cooked in coconut milk, served with relishes of roasted peanuts, *ikan bilis*, small salted fish the length of a fingernail, a hard boiled egg with perhaps some *rendang* or other curried meat and topped off with slices of cucumber. The whole concoction is assembled and wrapped into a pyramid shape in a piece of banana leaf, which keeps it moist and adds to the flavour, and when unwrapped serves as a plate. McDonald's eat your heart out! But Malaysians have been modernized. So, while *nasi lemak* can still be found in its original wrapping, the most common sight is people walking from hawker stalls complete with their *bungkus*: the word literally means parcel, but is now the term for a takeaway. The food is wrapped in waxed brown paper, parcelled up and secured with a rubber band and then put into a plastic bag; the waxed paper serves as your plate but adds nothing to the flavour. If you buy a drink it is poured directly into a plastic bag, whether it is an iced drink or piping hot, like a luscious *teh tarik*, pulled tea, a concoction rich in condensed milk and sugar that is mixed by pouring it from one container into another. The further apart the hawker holds the two containers, the longer the pull, the better the mix and the performance. Once the drink is in the plastic bag, one corner of this package is then bunched together and secured with a looped piece of coloured plastic string; this ingenious arrangement provides an opening into which a straw can be slotted for easy drinking and an convenient means of carrying. A refreshment run from any office can be accomplished by just one person, who will return with numerous drinks and packages of food suspended from their fingers. Your drink will hang safely and neatly from the slightly opened corner of a drawer and local tastebuds will be satisfied. Whatever you buy anywhere in KL will be encased in numerous layers of plastic bags, and richly stapled. The staple is a staple of even hawker stalls, where certain dishes, especially packages of the appropriate side relish, will be presented *bungkus* in stapled plastic bags. Like picking bones from one's fish, always be sure to carefully remove the staples before or during eating! At times I long for the ways of *nasi lemak*.

The daily transformation of Bangsar's main dining street gradually gave way to a more radical transformation into the yuppified, postmodern realms of nouveau Asian chic. The layout of the roads remained exactly as they had been but the buildings were, section by section, totally rebuilt in stylish fashion. The shops reopened transformed to cater for an international clientele of the discerning and not so discerning nouveau riche. An art gallery, antique shops aplenty, selling genuine antiques and real fakes produced by living antique modern artisans whose skill at imitation and ageing confounds even acknowledged art experts, or straightforward genuine imitation reproductions, and bric-à-brac shops of modish household ornament and accessory. These shops make a fetish of overpricing with profligate abandon. And between these high-price, high-end sales outlets began to congregate new eateries, the themed designer dining places offering Mexican, Mediterranean, Turkish, Chinese vegetarian, Indian vegetarian and local fusion cuisine. The final touch was the further transformation of one corner lot into a champagne and oyster bar open to the street on three levels. It is directly across the road from an unreconstructed Chinese restaurant that keeps on serving and selling in the old style. However, it was not lost on the owners that they were an anachronism. Their sumptuous feasts from an extensive menu covering the entire gamut of Chinese cuisine could be had at old-fashioned prices. The new eateries jostling around them, regularly changing hands, nationalities and styles of cuisine, had strictly limited menus and exorbitant prices. Looking for the win–win option the Chinese restaurant began to increase its prices. This occasioned outcries from the customers who work on the premise of local fare, local price, even if the next night they would go to one of the yuppie restaurants and have half the quantity and quality for triple the price and not bat an eye. Bangsar, like Petaling Street and many other areas of KL, accommodates contradiction, confusion and change with preservation and perseverance. The fully yuppified eateries of Bangsar are the chic place to hang out late into the night. The hawker stalls were banished to a great covered enclave popularly known as the jolly green giant, from its easily visible green tiled roof. It does roaring trade all day. After dark, resistance occupies the street outside the 'green giant'. Visible, indeed, directly across the road from the oyster bar standing on its corner of a four-way junction, is the night market of hawker food stalls, as they always were. Not forgotten, not neglected, appropriately foetid in traditional style, and amply attended into the small hours of the morning, long after the chic eateries have closed and their clientele of revellers have decided they need real sustenance.

The hills of Bangsar are a major hub of the resident expat community of all nationalities and the newly emergent Malaysian middle class. KL is in the Klang valley, off-centre of course, but this valley is bestrewn with hills. Not single up-and-down hills, but areas of deeply enfolded steep ravines. Bangsar is a network of ravines all built up with middle-class housing. The main road, Jalan Maroof, goes straight up, over and down. One turning leads into the yuppified shopping and eating domain; others lead into unimagined enclaves of twisting, turning streets of smart housing. Driving along the main road or the principal feeder streets you get no idea that whole enclaves lurk quietly out of sight behind them. KL is rather like Dr Who's Tardis, I sometimes think, larger on the inside than is visible from the outside. Jalan Maroof ends at a major junction where it meets a highway. From this highway you get to see the pinnacle of Bangsardom: Bukit Bandaraya, or as a friend of mine christened it 'Dato Elias's Revenge'. This one hill and its network of ravines is encrusted with wall-to-wall, cheek-by-jowl condominiums that are the antithesis of town planning. Dato Elias was the mayor of KL during this outbreak of speculative development. I once visited a hugely expensive penthouse apartment, an older development on the opposite side of Jalan Maroof from Bukit Bandaraya. From the balcony of the 21st floor one could look directly into the windows of a new condominium block rising on the other side of the road! Why did all the buildings congregate at this point? Bangsar is a fashionable address, especially for the expatriate community whose subsidized keeping-up of appearances sets the pace for local upwardly mobile aspiration. The area, its elevation bringing the dream of cool breezes, offers spectacular views created by the complex geology. From many a house perched on the edge of a ravine one can get breath-taking views of KL. So every property speculator dreamed of building a condo on this prime location and all appear to have been permitted to realize their dream, so the most common view from the apartments is another wall of windows and balconies glaring back at you. But the forecourt will have a stunning vista.

Across the road junction where Jalan Maroof terminates rise the hills of Damansara, another desirable address. From the junction you can see the undistinguished forbidding presence of the congealed blocks of government ministries, one of the two civil service hubs of the city, the other being the Kompleks Kerajaan, the government complex, on Jalan Duta. KL would never do something so out of character as to have just one administrative district. Their presence explains a good deal of the more restrained residential elegance of Damansara. More hills and ravines and twisted turns into enclaves one could not have imagined existed. This is middle-class KL en masse in their bungalow houses, bungalow being the term for a detached house that is almost invariably of two storeys. As new areas of this once publicly owned land were opened up for development, plots were balloted among civil servants. I once met an Indian couple who explained how the system worked. They

Damansara Housing Development: 'middle-class KL en masse in their bungalow houses'.

had spent their entire working lives in government service, the health service; both were doctors, earning modest salaries even by pre-rampant economic growth standards. Even steady, unspectacular growth, however, made facility for redistribution. The ballots recognized years of service and enabled the couple to obtain two prime lots of land in Damansara on which they could build houses. As economic growth, land and property prices spiralled they were rather taken aback to find themselves with assets of considerable worth, and humbly beholden for their good fortune. The system was patronage, but, when you reflect on its social effects, it was patronage with a heart of gold. Modestly paid public service was attended with a whole network of entitlements and perks, which long into rampant growth meant people were better off not switching to the private sector. It meant that Malaysia had an effective civil administration as the backbone of its planned development activities and these civil servants had a share in the rising standards of living and expectation their careers underpinned. 'Face' is an essential ethos in Asia; 'giving face', according people honour and respect, is as important as not 'losing face', being disrespected and offended. There is a great deal of acceptable face about KL, solid dignified achievement and character. Imaginary visions of the exotic Orient and latter-day visions of impoverished Third World backwaters all fail to grasp the reality of KL. The graceful bungalows of Damansara, the postmodern abundance of the Mall and – yes – the enclaves of squatter houses are all there. They have subtle and real interconnections, tense but sustainable bonds, sensitive relations of hard bargaining and trade-offs – all of which means that like the physical space they occupy they are bigger on the inside than they look on the surface.

Damansara is the place to find 'datodom' in earnest: an address that bespeaks and invokes the pervasive system of symbols of social status – titles. In Malaysia, status means more than having money; it means having memory. The national memory is given physical manifestation in terms of titles and honours. Since the quickest route to obtaining such decorations is via hereditary royalty, civil service or politics, the Malays have made these their special preserves. Over half of all the kings in the world are in Malaysia: nine at the last count! Every five years they get together and elect a grand king (the Agong) from amongst themselves; the Agong would then take up residence in the national palace located in KL. The remaining time is spent awarding countless titles to each other, members of the civil service and anyone else who is anxious to acquire them or able to buy them. His Majesty the Yang DiPertuan Agong, the elected king of Malaysia as a whole, as well as all the 'rulers' of all the states, such as Duli Yang Maha Mulia Sultan Yang DiPertuan Bagi Negeri dan Jajahan Johoree – His Royal Highness the Sultan and Sovereign of the State and Territory of Johore – hand out orders and decorations by the truck-load. The titles come in a strict hierarchy and Malays take the protocol of hierarchy very seriously. A few years ago I found myself addressing a conference. Within minutes of beginning my disquisition, there was a commotion on the podium and an invited dignitary made a ceremonial exit. It transpired he was a Tun (a kind of trebled 'Sir') but was seated, by an oversight, in a lower ranking than a Dato (a mere single 'Sir') and he found the insult to his social status too much to bear. The titles, orders and awards, which encapsulate the entire history of Malaya, come in four basic varieties – royal and family orders, chivalrous orders, gallantry decorations and medals of achievement – and a number of different grades. The royal and family orders have titles like Darjah Yang Maha Utama Kerabat Diraja Malaysia (The Most Excellent Order of the Royal Family of Malaysia) or DKM for short; and Darjah Utama Seri Mahkota Negara (The Most Exalted Order of the Crown of the Realm), or DMN for short. Orders of chivalry come in various varieties and classes with titles like Darjah Yang Amat Dihormati Setia Diraja (The Most Honourable Royal Order of Loyalty), First Class: Panglima Setia DiRaja, PSD (Commander). Gallantry decorations have the most colourful of all titles: Seri Pahwalwan Gagan Perkasa – SP (Gallant and Brave Warrior), Panglima Gagah Berani – PGB

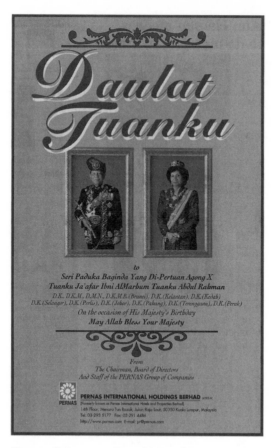

The appellation game in its highest form: an advertisement from the *New Straits Times*.

(Brave and Daring), Kepujian Perutusan Keberranian – KPK (Mention-in-Despatches). More important in contemporary currency is the fact these honours come with titles such as Tun, Tan Sri, Dato Sri and Dato: anyone who is anyone in Kuala Lumpur sports one or many of these titles; anyone who wants to become someone seeks vigorously to acquire a set. Those who have acquired the exalted status of Dato or Tan Tri spend a great deal of energy informing the whole country that they have arrived. One of the most common sights in local newspapers are advertisements either congratulating someone on acquiring a title or thanking this or that Dato, complete with an official picture, for doing this or that nothing. Thus, the owners of a shopping mall, or a factory, or a condominium, will show their gratitude to a minister for 'opening' their commodity by taking out a full-page advertisement in the *New Strait Times*, the *Star* and the *Malay Mail*, thanking

Dato Sri Paduka Shahabuddin bin Mohammad Ali DPMP, SPNS, SPMK, DPMK, SSSA, SPSK, DKYR, SPNS, SIMP, SPCM, SPMT, DP.

Very old Malay tradition is delicately transmuted to serve the changed realities of society and economy: Chinese and Indian politicians and businessmen also acquire their full complement of awards and titles. All acquire and retain the sensitivities appropriate to hierarchy. In the minefield of titles there is a simple expedient – if in doubt, give face. This means if you are unsure whether someone has a title call them Dato; if you are unsure which grade call them Tan Sri – Tuns are too few and too exalted, so never flirt with the realms of such hyperbole. Only if you are absolutely certain refer to anyone as a common or garden Encik, Mr, or Cik, Madam. With Malays you can always subvert and cut through the entire edifice by referring to someone as the always acceptable Hajji or Hajjah, the honorific for someone who has performed the pilgrimage to Mecca. Giving face means always more, never less, and is a formality that denotes respect for the worth of the person as a person worthy of honour; thus all people can in some sense be greeted as lords and ladies.

III

Negotiating the complex minefield of titles is only one of many social problems in KL. Making sense of the local lingo is another. When Malaysians speak, they may speak in Malay, Chinese or Tamil. But virtually everyone also speaks English, or a kind of English that is all their own. This Malaysian English operates within a Malay, Chinese or Tamil mental framework and is generously peppered with a free-floating vocabulary of, in themselves, meaningless words. The most common of these words is *lah* that, so far as my two decades of intensive research has shown, is an audio version of the exclamation mark. Malaysians tend to express surprise, emotion, enthusiasm, regret, contempt, command, wonder, admiration, absurdity, boredom and much else besides by adding a *lah* at the end of a sentence. So, for example, while a shopper in London may cry 'How expensive!' or simply 'Cheap!', a Malaysian will declare, 'So expensive-*lah*' or 'So cheap-*lah*'. There is a rhyme and a pattern to the use of *lah*; it is not just to be thrown in at the end of any sentence. It gives spoken Malaysian English a rhythm and an authenticity all its own. A brother of *lah* is the *ah*. The *ah* has a whole hue of meanings depending on how and where it is used. A simple but indifferent 'thank you' can be transformed into an ever so polite and concerned 'thank you-*ah*'. In addition to the *lah* and *ah*, Malaysian English incorporates a whole range of equivalent words from the vernacular languages. The Malaysian equivalent for 'yes' is actually the Malay *boleh, boleh,* or the Cantonese *tuck, tuck,* or the Hokkien *eh sai, eh sai* – all of which are translated as 'can'. So to a simple question, 'can I do this', the Malaysian answer would be 'can, can' or 'can-*lah*' or a full-blown *boleh-lah*. It could also be 'can not' or 'can not-*lah*', or even 'donno', or the original *ta'k boleh*. For the same reason, you are never taken anywhere, you are always sent ('I will send you home, *lah*'); one is always 'on'ing' and 'off'ing' things ('on the radio-*lah*', 'off the volume-*lah*') and showing 'face'. For similar reasons, the syntax is also jumbled up and the pronouns always appear at the end of the sentence. Malay language works by categorizing things, from the most general and inclusive through to a ranking of lesser generality that eventually and in combination define a specific and individual form. It is a language that traces its historic roots and interconnectivity with many loan words from other languages, including Arabic, Persian and Urdu – the ones I am familiar with. The romanization of the language provides endless delights to the spellingly challenged. Science, avoiding all 'i before e' complexity, becomes 'sains'. A friend of mine always repeats her lame joke about 'secular' buses. Bus, according to Malay phonetic values, becomes *bas*. Why, she always asks, in a country that is reputed to be strongly Islamic, do you see so many 'secular' *bas-bas*? And here in Kuala Lumpur they are bright yellow and everywhere on the road: *Bas Sekolah*. The joke turns on the variation of phonetic values from English. In Malay and to Malaysian English *sekolah* spells and says 'scholar', hence school bus. To make a plural in Malay one repeats a word, so schools would be *sekolah-sekolah*. Writing plurals on billboards and signs, however, is laborious and space consuming so an ingenious adaptation has been made. A purveyor of goods, which should be *barang-barang*, will be signposted as purveyor of *barang* squared, using the mathematical symbol, thus: *barang²*. The invariable introduction process at formal functions becomes *Tun Tun, Tan Sri Tan Sri, Dato Dato, Tuan Tuan dan Puan Puan*, descending through the realms of status to the common or garden gentleman and lady, *tuan* and *puan*, in amply plural form but never squared.

The harmonics of the local language turn into a delight when one is out and about in the streets of KL, the arteries of the city. The business heart of the city is the area around Sungei Wang Plaza, Jalan Rajah Chulan and Jalan Sultan. Jalan Sultan, a pernicious stretch of snail's pace, has been designated the thoroughfare of five-star hotels, either already built and long in operation or in various stages of construction and completion. Five-star is the status Prime Minister Mahathir sought for everything, budget tourists not really wanted or needing to apply. Five-star tourists require five-star shopping complexes to service their place in the scheme of things, making Kuala Lumpur a premiere shopping holiday destination. So tourists add to the traffic and bustle of a business district that is not only burgeoning five-star hotels but also new five-star office complexes in marble and glass that look like five-star hotels. From the windows of a room in the long-established KL Hilton on Jalan Sultan, you used to be able to get a superb view of the old racecourse. It was set out green and pleasant where the land fell away behind the hill on which stands the hotel and also the old shopping complex of Sungei Wang. The racecourse has been relocated and the area now houses the most five-star edifice of them all, KLCC, the Kuala Lumpur City Centre development that is also known as the Petronas Twin Towers, the tallest building in the world. Alone, in and of itself, KLCC has enough shops and offices to fit an entire business city within. But it is only the biggest among many. When designated for development the whole area became known as the Golden Triangle. The invocation of the ill-gotten and unsavoury activities of another location also known as the Golden Triangle was neither entirely innocent nor inadvertent in the pithy parlance of KL. Sungei Wang Plaza predates all this resplendence: it is one of the oldest shopping complexes in the city. In fact, it isn't one but two shopping malls rolled into one maze-like conglomerate. Sungei Wang Plaza backs directly into Bukit Bintang Plaza – so one can wander seamlessly from one to the other without actually realizing that shopping boundaries have been crossed. Across the road, but linked by a green bridge, is a third plaza, a recent addition from the boom years: Lot 10. So close, yet Lot 10 is world apart from Sungei Wang.

Sungei Wang is essentially a Chinese enclave. The moment you step in you are greeted by an extraordinary, slightly pungent, somewhat sickly smell. It is almost impossible to place. It took me numerous visits before I realized that it is a combination of burnt skin (from cosmetic surgery), a loose amalgam of hair products, the thin slivers of roast pork called *bak wah* and Peking duck. It is very easy to get lost in this complex, particularly when it is always being renovated. I often pay a visit to patronize Madame Chan's Reflexology Centre on the first floor. When I first saw Madame Chan she was sitting, as she usually is, behind an official-looking desk sipping herbal tea. 'Welcome', she said as she saw me approach. 'Not looking good today, *lah*', she announced as I pulled up a chair and sat in front of her. 'You tired, sleepless nights-*ah*! Back pain. Reflexology-*ah*, very good for back pain, insomnia, amenorrhoea.'

'Amenorrhoea? What's that?'

'Oh, that's when menstruation goes missing, *lah*.' She paused to think and realized her mistake. 'Ah, ah', she laughed, 'wrong sex-*ah*'. She paused again and then continued. 'But reflexology good for men too. Helps in relaxing. Good for people like you, tired and emotional. Even help dick action, *lah*.'

'Dick action? Yes, I can certainly do with some help in that direction!', I murmured as she handed me her card. I read: 'Madame Chan, expert in ancient Chinese art of reflexology. Helps relaxation, back pain, headaches, migraine and dig astion. Opening hours: 10–8; Sundays: Close at 7.'

'Oh, digestion. You got me a little confused, Madame Chan', I said. 'You had me thinking in other directions.'

'Helps confusion too', Madame Chan replied with a straight face. 'Helps in all directions, *lah*.' She got up and ushered me to an armchair. 'Come sit here. Close your eyes and relax-*ah*.'

As I made myself comfortable on the armchair, Madame Chan took my feet, removed my shoes and socks, washed my feet with a water spray and began massaging with a herbal wax. It had a gentle, pleasant smell, rather like Chinese tea. Every now and again she would use a wooden pick-like device to pummel away at awkward parts of the sole and knowingly opine, 'it hurts at the spine, *lah*, the left shoulder's bit stiff, *lah* . . .' Then her comments changed gear; she began to inform me: 'You had your appendices out, *lah*, you have constipation, *lah*, your left eye needs attention, *lah* . . .'

The reflexology sessions normally last forty minutes. I would always leave Madame Chan's Centre aching but feeling as though I was floating on air. Once, when in masochistic mood, I walked down to the basement of Sungei Wang and wandered into a Chinese medicine shop to be greeted warmly by a slender Chinese man with a wispy beard. He took my hand and announced that I looked a bit stiff.

'Stiff?'

'Yes-*ah*! Stiff. Joints not moving, *lah*, not much relax.'

'But I've just had a reflexology session. I feel great.'

'Yes, *lah*! Reflexology good. Make blood circulation. But you too much *yin*, *lah*! You exhausted and weak.'

He goes on to explain that I am sustained by *chi* that circulates inside my body. This force should be balanced; the elements (wood, fire, earth, metal and water) should be in harmony. But sometimes there is too much *yin* (female, dark, moist, yielding) or too much *yang* (male, bright, warm and demanding). When *yang* rules, a person becomes hyperactive and angry. When *yin* rules, exhaustion sets in. He takes my pulse for what seems like ages and then analyses the state of various organs in my body. Finally, he writes down a prescription and hands it to one of his assistants. While the assistant starts to measure out the various herbs and roots and much else besides, the doctor explains that he wants to treat my whole body, not just the symptoms. His treatments do not bring about immediate relief or dramatic improvement but will be the start of a long-term personal health programme, a programme that involves serious responsibility on my part. When the prescription is ready, I receive a large bag of ingredients. I am asked to boil the contents thoroughly and drink the resulting soup. Just before I was about to leave the shop, the doctor called me back.

'You also need healthy balls', he says. 'They nice to look at and can do you more healthy. And give quick help for circulation of blood, *lah*.' He placed two heavy onyx balls in my hand. 'Put balls in one hand, move balls with five fingers.'

I began to manipulate the smooth balls with my wrist.

'Work of craftsmen-*ah*!'

I nodded in agreement. He explained.

'On the basis of Chinese medical theory, "ten fingers connecting heart", the main and collateral channels in your hands connect your brain and viscera. When you move the balls, they can stimulate the passage to your hands, through which vital energy circulate. By practising it can stimulate the circulation of blood and cause muscles and joints to relax, *lah*. It works for avoiding hypertension and chronic disease. If you practise

The great green edifice: 'Lot 10 is my idea of hell.'

regularly strengthens memory, remove fatigue and prolong life, *lah*.' I pay for the healthy balls and exit rapidly.

The change in atmosphere from Sungei Wang and Bukit Bintang Plazas to Lot 10 is akin to the mental gymnastics needed to switch from Chinese medicine to the Western, allopathic one. Lot 10 caters largely for the rich upper crust of the Malaysian society. It is Kuala Lumpur's equivalent of London's Knightsbridge or New York's Fifth Avenue. But there is a major difference. There are no finicky rules against rucksacks or shellsuits (especially those worn by weight-challenged Americans) or looking scruffy. Lot 10 is anything but haughty; like Malaysian corruption, it is thoroughly democratic. No one wandering into Lot 10 will meet the fate of Julia Roberts in *Pretty Woman*. In a memorable scene she tried purchase from the likes of Chanel, Giorgio and Fendi on Rodeo Drive, Los Angeles, but was ostracized because she looked like the penniless hooker she was. Later in the film, when flush and fully made over thanks to Richard Gere's cash, she went back to these stores for every shopper's dream revenge. 'You work on commission, right?', she says to a startled sales assistant. 'Big mistake', she notes as she brandishes boxes and bags full of high-price merchandise acquired elsewhere. And leaves in triumph. In Lot 10, shoppers can enter flash shops, examine the exuberant goods on exhibit, try on what takes their fancy and walk out

111

dreaming of the day they will win the lottery. Shop assistants in Lot 10 treat every customer, no matter how penniless he or she looks, with equal courtesy and potential. Some of the customers here remind me of the character played by Margaret Rutherford in the 1950s English comedy, *Trouble in Store*. She bought an occasional item or two but her main objective was to so overwhelm the sales assistants with her aristocratic mien and grand manner that they do not notice that she was shoplifting. Indeed, she even got the staff to help her carry her ill-gotten gains outside to a waiting taxi. But at Lot 10, I have never actually seen anyone steal. Indeed, before the late 1990s economic crisis put desperation on the streets, crime was feared and visibly guarded against – all houses are encrusted with embedded wrought iron grilles and Chinese homes have vicious guard dogs that disturb the night at every rustle and the passage of every creature – but not very common. Indeed Kuala Lumpur is infinitely safer than London, light years and galaxies safer than New York. When a British friend's visiting mother had her purse pinched at Lot 10 I have never seen such consternation among the sales assistants, security staff and other order of attendants who quickly appeared on the scene. They were genuinely shocked and upset; they all apologized profusely, as if the entire nation had lost face, which in their estimation it had. And all this over a purse that contained hardly any money and had inadvertently been left unattended in an open handbag, out of sight of the entire party.

IV

Lot 10, for all the humanity of the sales assistants, is my idea of hell. The very name has connotations of a cemetery, unwittingly suggesting that shopping can be deadly. Indeed, the developments sprouting all over the ever-expanding business district have become quite deadly, way past the balance and harmony beloved of the purveyors of traditional medicine in all the cultural varieties so readily available in KL, the Chinese, Indian

Ayurvedic and traditional Malay. The entire area seems to be suffering from hypertension and in need of stimulating its passage to a new system of long-term personal health programmes based on more serious personal responsibility. When the East Asian economic crisis hit KL it was this district that showed the worst signs of chronic disease, for all its marble, glass and stainless steel elegance. The main road became the abandoned building site of the elevated monorail. KL is a city with rudimentary public transport. There are buses, and efforts were made to upgrade from the old exhaust fume-belching pink variety to more modern fuel-efficient air-conditioned varieties. There are taxis everywhere and they used to be cheap and efficient. Only in the final phase of the boom did one have to endure the very un-KL like problems of sharks and charlatans behind the wheel. But the taxi drivers became frenzied in response to a situation they had not created. The arteries of the roads, always being renovated and upgraded, were always clogged with more and more vehicles meaning that one small fare could take a taxi driver hours to earn. So they began negotiating prices according to route, time of day and concomitant wear and tear on nervous system and blood pressure as well as earning capacity.

It is easy to become aware that KL is bigger on the inside than it appears. It takes a specific calendrical conjunction to learn that KL, despite all its various hubs, is actually quite a small place. Getting from anywhere to anywhere within this city befuddles one's sense of direction. It look me a long time to realize that Sungei Wang Plaza is located just up the hill from Chinatown. Or that one could just continue all the way up Jalan Tunku Abdul Rahman and round a corner to be on Jalan Sultan, admittedly some distance from where it begins to sprout five-star hotels. This route enables you to make a great loop, passing Sungei Wang Plaza, to bring you back to Chinatown. Travelling in the other direction you can take a short cut to Damansara via the Lake Gardens, the wonderful park that now houses not only a pretty lake but a bird park, an orchid garden, a butterfly park and deer park as well as the National Monument. Built in imitation of

Seri Carcosa, the Governor's residence, *c. 1897*. Anyone can go there now to take 'high tea'.

the famous photograph of American soldiers raising the flag on Iwo Jima, the monument is set out with colonnades and fountains on the highest promontory of the Lake Gardens. It is just above the garden of ASEAN symbolic sculptures, one donated by each member country of the Association of South East Asian Nations, which is visible from the road. The view from the monument is spectacular – the city buried in trees. Standing out on a nearby hill, just about to reintegrate with the forest, is the colonial splendour of Seri Carcosa, the mansion that used to be the governor general's residence. It is now a hotel beyond five-star rating, although anyone can visit to take high tea and sample the ambience. There is something magical about the way KL seems to expand and contract as one attempts to get from one part of the city to another. It retains straight-to-the-point back roads that go directly from one hub to another. It is constantly acquiring imposing networks of six-lane highways and flyovers always under construction, permanently under renovation that go in wide swinging loops round and about to end up half a mile from where you started out. It's only the amount of traffic that makes it seems a long distance because it takes such a time to get everywhere by any road. This magical mystery of space in time is made apparent when Chinese New Year and Hari Raya coincide.

Why do Chinese New Year and Hari Raya make a difference, and why do they not always coincide so that space and time can be reunited? Christmas and New Year are fixed points in the calendar, occasions with the programmed, routinized thoroughness of industrialized Western society. Asian festivals, taking their cue from lunar cycles, have a delightful tendency to wander around the Gregorian calendar. I remember once sitting in the coffee shop of the Pan Pacific Hotel on New Year's Day watching one harassed female supervise an army of decorative display operatives taking down the Christmas trees and polystyrene snowflakes to replace them instantaneously with cherry blossom boughs and pussy willow canes. Equatorial heat can do that, you know, turn winter to spring, the promise of Chinese New Year, in the twinkling of an eye. Chinese New Year can occur anytime between early January and late February. In recent years the moon of Chinese New Year began to coincide with the moon signalling the beginning of Ramadan according to the Muslim lunar calendar. Inexorably, as the years passed and the Muslim lunar calendar marched forward eleven days each year, Chinese New Year began to coincide with Hari Raya. In polite KL society this multicultural conjunction demanded some sensitive handling. Malaysians do not just decorate for festivals, do not merely observe them – they celebrate them. Multiculturalism is not a tourist ploy, nor a notional idea to which lip service is paid – it is a lived reality. Chinese New Year is an outpouring of mandarin oranges and food hampers wrapped in foil containing every goody imaginable, with prominent pride of place going to XO brandy. Shops will be replete with bright red decorative hangings, and have lettuce suspended above their doorways, awaiting the arrival of lion dance troupes who will perform their elaborate dance, accompanied by booming drums, until the lion stretches up and grasps the lettuce in its jaws. The whole procedure ensures the arrival of good fortune and scares off evil spirits for the coming year, as do the vicious firecrackers people let off, despite everyone agreeing they are dangerous and not strictly legal. Learning from the Malays, every community has acquired the habit of the open house, inviting the neighbours, friends or any passers-by to drop in to share in the feast. But during Ramadan the entire Malay community is focused on the spiritual discipline of fasting from dawn to dusk. To help them in their efforts non-Muslim Malaysians engage in a shared game of avoidance; many politely decline to eat and drink in public mixed company and hide out of sight and down wind to have a smoke. So what to do when Chinese New Year occurs during Ramadan? With practised adroitness Chinese open houses became evening affairs, after the breaking of the fast, so Muslim friends can call in and share the fun.

Four years later there was another problem – how to keep KL running when Chinese New Year and Hari Raya, both two-day holidays, occurred in the same week. For a few years the two lunar calendars coincided. The upshot was that the whole country was on holiday and in festive mood, not that you would know if you were in Kuala Lumpur. It became a ghost city, a post-apocalyptic scene of empty wind-blown streets with a few surviving joyless stragglers scavenging for provisions. It is at such times one realizes how shallow is the urban experience in the history of Malaysians. Yes, all the people were at home celebrating. It's just that to accomplish this communal festive exercise they *balai kampung*, really go home, to the villages around the peninsula from which they came to reside and work in the city. For days the bus and train stations and the airport were a sea of people on the move. All roads out of the city had been solid walls of traffic heading 'out station', as the local saying goes. After the whirlwind came the unnatural calm; the eye of the festival passed over the slumbering city, where you could walk unafraid down the middle of the highways. This was the time I had ease and leisure to find out how small, with all its

Balai kampung. During Hari Raya and Chinese New Year the residents of Kuala Lumpur desert the city for the *kampungs* of their birth.

internal bigness, KL actually is. I whizzed around, feeling magically transported through sections of KL that normally mean delays of up to an hour, to visit other lonely leftover city dwellers.

The eye of the festival passes, but there is no accompanying clamour to return. The festival, if you will, is a process, a two-month process. During Ramadan the usual Malay hawker stalls around the city will be closed, not being needed during daytime hours, and all stalls will look rather lonely and less patronized. But whole new areas of hawker stalls, the *kueh* stalls, will open up. This is the best time of year to examine and sample Malay food at its finest. By mid-afternoon people will start trickling towards the *kueh* stalls, becoming a heaving crowd as the last hours of daylight wind towards sundown. Throngs of people mill around to select the special items they will take home and savour at break-fast. Hotels and restaurants will be crowded for break-fast buffets. Malays will pile their plates and select the special drink concoctions of their choice, then sit patiently with mounds of food before them waiting for the gong, or drum roll and sound of the call to prayer before touching a mouthful. Formal gatherings for the collective breaking of fast are arranged by companies, organizations, institutions and prominent individuals. And after the food there are prayers. Some of these gatherings will organize *traweeh* prayers. Ramadan commemorates the process of revelation of the Qur'an to the Prophet Muhammad; *traweeh* prayers mean reciting the whole of the Qur'an, during the last prayer of the day, over the course of the month. So for Malays, and by implication everyone else, the daily rhythm of KL life changes for the entire month. Then comes Hari Raya, a collective letting out of breath and settling in to some serious thanksgiving, hospitality and recommitment to family, community and friends. The first and second days of Hari Raya are the first and second days of the month of Shawwal; according to Malays during this month you should try to visit and be visited by everyone you know – hence the institution of the open house. So from *kampung* back to the city is a meandering journey of reacquaintance, a holiday season. After a month of effort, working while fasting, there is a leisurely recuperation before picking up the pace again.

In KL it became the norm to receive invitations to organized open houses spread throughout the month of Shawwal. One should not be confused by the system of invitations, the between-this-and-this-hour: open houses are genuinely open. I remember sitting in the garden of a friend's home when a group of visitors arrived overcome with mirth. They had spent the last hour at a house across the street enjoying open house before they realized they were at the wrong address! No one objected. No one minded. They felt obligated to change location merely to ensure they did actually greet their intended hosts. The hawkers reappear and do roaring business during Shawwal. In very KL fashion the local authority has an agency that enables people to hire particular hawkers and their speciality fare for any function, and open houses are the ultimate function in posh KL circles. One arrives at people's homes to find their garden has been transformed into a mini Bangsar: just wander around and take your pick.

Chinese New Year, like Hari Raya, is not just a two-day holiday but fifteen days of appropriate activities from the New Year to Chap Goh Mai, from the family dinner, the receiving of visitors to the honouring of the family ancestors. The conjunction of festivals puts inordinate pressure on the catering industry and hotels that must find the resources and rooms to service all the functions at which individuals and organizations share their festivities with everyone else. It will be a long time before Hari Raya and Chinese New Year coincide again. Hari Raya continues its course through the Gregorian calendar to meet up with Christmas, before moving on to coincide with Deepavali, sometime during late October or early November some year soon. None of the subsequent conjunctions will transmute KL into quite such a ghost town. But they do present commodified quandaries, which customers to woo, which marketing and decorative traditions to pander to. A genuinely multicultural world is full of questions, delicate questions, and delicate sensibilities.

119

The serial conjunction of different calendars occasion many intercommunal adjustments. There are twelve zodiac years in the Chinese cycle, such as the year of the rabbit and the rat. But in Malaysia only, the Chinese year of the pig becomes the year of the boar, Malays having a great horror of the pig. Genuine, operative multiculturalism is about living with differences, not all of which are welcome. All Malaysians discuss them openly in terms that horrify the politically correct discourse of those who come from less accommodating multicultural domains. The open, too-honest nitpicking is part of the realism that makes multiculturalism genuine and problematic, a positive strength, not merely an unfortunate, unavoidable, grudging fact. The multiculturalism one finds in KL is a hard bargain, a recognized problem, one that has been crafted out of difficult, contested choices. It gives predominance to the majority Malay Muslim community and their language and cultural traditions, and then secures, not just in decorative but real living terms, the guaranteed continuity of Chinese and Indian language and culture, all rounded off with a stake in political power for all communities. It took a long time to build the only working multicultural society on earth, and already it has outgrown its infancy – the gerrymandered political communalism. It has developed only to be denied its adult maturity – genuinely internalized national acceptance operated through individual responsibility – by the very political dispensation that gave it birth and room to grow. Communalism is a power structure of vested interests that has its dark side and its debilities as well as its positive lived reality. Even so, Malaysia seems to have learned that multiculturalism is easy to talk about but that as a sustainable lived reality it is hard work. Differences are real and substantive and need sensitivity because we are all sensitive about who we are, where we come from and how we feel we should live, the place distinct traditions should occupy in our individual lives and in the organization of our society at large. And, at the end of the day we all want everything, all tradition, all history, all modernity, all choice, and all their contradictions. Living with juxtaposition and contradiction is an endlessly perplexing undertaking. In KL everyone, and especially the Malays, seems to flirt with being subsumed, homogenized and celebrated into a postmodern eclectic virtual reality, becoming the programmed consumers consumed by the commodification of everything. Yet, somehow, by this very ploy they dig their heels in and stubbornly maintain their own sense of identity.

v

Postmodern juxtaposition and pastiche can be quite extreme. It can play havoc with even the strongest sense of identities. In KL, the Mall, Lot 10 and the endless chain of five-star hotels perform a particular kind of violence on the assumptions of Malay identity, in particular its source of sustenance, the notions of space and time.

The traditional Malays have always lived in proverbial harmony with their environment, and with a very strong sense of time rippling through space. We can see this in Malay arts, which draw their breath from the very atmosphere of the peninsula. In the art of gold thread weaving (*kain songket*), for example, the stitching has names like clouds in procession (*awan berarak*), swirling eddy (*air muleh*), chain of bays (*teluk berantai*), seahorse (*unduk-unduk*), bamboo shoot (*pucuk rebung*) and cock's tail (*lawi muleh*). There is also a strong relationship between time and space. Thus, 'free time' is associated with 'open space': the very traditional terms for free time, *masa lapang* or *masa luang*, actually mean open or unused spaces. Even though the Malays did not develop instruments for measuring time, they used a whole variety of calendars to keep track of time – the lunar calendar of Islam, the twelve-year cycles of the Chinese zodiac, or *kop*, as well as the *daur kecil* of the Malays and the *windu* system of the Javanese. In all these systems, time, nature and space are linked; the interconnection is intrinsic to the traditional Malay worldview. The new truncated spaces – boxed condominiums, perpendicular, insular hotels – deliver a double whammy: they break the umbilical cord between space and nature and chop time into discrete units. The symmetrical relationship between space and time is transformed into an asymmetrical one.

In the round but asymmetrical lobbies of five-star hotels, one can order a rather rich club sandwich. This giant, multilayered meal is almost as appetizing as colonialism, to which it has more than a passing resemblance. If the bread at the bottom has been cooked with colonial history, the upper layer is now being manufactured by postmodernism. The bread in between is a product of modernity and the generous filling is all that remains of Malay tradition and culture. The recipe with which modernity cooked, for example, 'Malay folk literature' is now being used to season the Malay mind. Malay folk literature, as we understand it today, is a product of British Orientalism. The well-meaning British started to collect folk literature without knowing anything about oral cultures or bothering to study oral modes of composition. They simply chose what they thought should be recorded from various dialects; and the Malays recorded it. Sometimes the Malays objected, particularly when they were forced to record material they thought was not worth preserving, such as the local numbskull stories (Pak Pandir tales, the equivalent of Irish jokes, or if you are Irish, Kerryman jokes). Both the colonial British and the modern Malays saw the traditional storytellers, who could induce a hypnotic spell in the listeners, as a threat – a threat to reason, a threat to the rationalized sanity of society. The intimacy between the teller and the told was too potentially explosive and combustible a mix both for colonialism and modernity. The traditional storyteller, like the *dalit* of the *wayang kulit* shadow play, is a natural satirist of the contemporary scene, a natural subversive. So, Malay folk literature had to be moved from its oral base to printed form. 'Authentic' *texts* became important, traditional tales were turned into 'literature', passages arbitrarily broken into 'lines' and printed as poetry, classical material rendered into romanized script and translated into English to give it gravitas. So, what was dynamic and evolving and an integral part of the consciousness of the Malays was frozen and solidified and divorced from much of society. Literature had a new meaning, a meaning that enveloped Malay history and tradition in Western modernity, a continuation of colonialism by another name.

The end product in both cases is cultural asymmetry. The dislocation of Malay folk literature as well as the displacement of Malay notions of space and time have generated minds that are totally out of sync with themselves. The most common sight in the Mall, and other shopping complexes in Kuala Lumpur, are the youth who go *lepak*. These are school children who loiter around looking bored out of their minds. In this jungle of brick and mortar, digital clocks and mobile phones, fast food and even faster 'rides', there is nothing real to hold on to. All experience is ephemeral; and there is no connection between what is said and done, what is believed and practised, what is sold and bought. The disenfranchising of the Malay minds from their own sense of space and time, from the folk traditions that enraptured and entertained them, is a form of self-inflicted colonialism. It can only produce, as the postmodern craze of going *lepak* and, as Malaysian pop lyrics demonstrate, highly perturbed minds. The consumers thus become those who are actually being consumed. Despite resistance, despite the infinite adaptability thesis, the innate acumen for the subtle accommodation of a multiculturalism beyond the imagination of postmodernism, the city is being eaten from the inside.

Magicians and Economic Miracles

I

In aerial photographs designed for tourists, Kuala Lumpur appears immersed in forest. Trees are everywhere and belie the existence of much of its developed urban space. At least, there remain areas of the city where this symbiosis continues to be true. The older mature parts of the city have been enveloped in a friendly, cooling and shady embrace by trees. But development is a stern taskmaster. Approach Kuala Lumpur from the air and you will see every environmental activist's nightmare. Between the extensive blanket of green, there seem to be open wounds, bald areas of land that have been stripped right down to the exposed soil. Open to the elements, the land begins as a dark reddish ochre and turns paler the longer it is exposed to the sun, getting a reverse suntan as the nutrients are leached from the soil by the rain. Travel often enough and you will be able to detect which bald patches are commercial estates being cleared for the planting of new rubber or palm oil saplings and those which are earmarked for development. On the palest wounds you gradually see the geometric incursions of roads and pipelines, then the foundations of housing estates emerge, then, in the blinking of an eye new suburbs sparkle in the sun. At ground level these developers' dreams of the good life are more like a nightmare. Uniform, standardized and not acclimatized, the houses owe their inspiration not to equatorial traditions of house building but some universal, homogenized suburbia with a hint of the Mediterranean. The entire layout, street after street, is dusty and strewn with the rubbish of construction; it feels like walking around inside a pressure cooker. A moment's pause and you realize what makes such places so alien, so vacuous, such caverns of empty desire – there are no trees.

124

Malaysians tend not to respond to environmental alarmism, though they are highly concerned and motivated on green issues. Stay long enough in the country and you begin to appreciate some of the reasons. Most residents of Kuala Lumpur are first-generation, migrants to the city in their own lifetime. They were born in *kampung*, sons and daughters of farmers, agricultural labourers, estate workers. They know better, more intimately, at first hand, how development degrades their environment, how the rivers in which as children they swam and bathed are becoming polluted. For Malaysians the fate of the environment is not an intellectual issue; it is a visceral sense of ill-ease. But then, Malaysians know more about the proclivities of their environment than the reductive ideas that are so commonplace among short-term expert visitors. The classic example they will point out is Krakatoa, the famous volcanic island that is not east of Java, as the title of a big-budget Hollywood disaster epic once claimed in cinemascope geographic incorrectness. Krakatoa is west of Java, but it did spectacularly explode early in this century in a

Tourist Malaysia is not just a travel agent's invention.

massive volcanic eruption that sent a frisson of nuclear winter around the globe, destroyed all life on the island and devastated the surrounding region. Sixty years on, the island has regenerated. By natural processes it is now a functional equatorial landscape again; trees and all kinds of plants and animals are back.

It is not just that Malaysians know the jungle cannot be kept at bay. Their complacency, if complacency it is, has been bred from their engagement with the jungle. All those leafy corners of Kuala Lumpur, developed as long ago as a decade or two, have not been embraced by nature unfettered and exuberantly left to its own devices. Put a Malaysian in any setting and they begin to interact with their environment in a deliberate way: they plant. 'Trees very cooling', people will tell you. And so they are. So the first thing a house needs is a pleasant, cooling encrustation of trees; then it needs flowers to bring bursts of colour to delight the eye. The trees will often be fruit trees such as banana and coconut, which serve a dual purpose since they are also dietary staples. Malays can work more culinary wonders with bananas than one can easily comprehend. *Pisang emas*, the golden banana, a small thin-skinned variety, one of the many named varieties available, has a taste unbeknownst to anyone reared on the chalky tasteless specimens found in shops in the West. Malays disseminated the banana to the rest of the world, but the delicate richness of the original just did not translate to other locations. Coconut palms rearing above houses provide the essential tropical touch to the city and the customary taste to local food. Then there are other fruit trees: papaya with its ornate foliage that grows rapidly and spawns offshoots readily in any garden; mango the fruit of which Malays love to eat unripened and hence acidic and tart with the accompaniment of a rich sauce in *rojak*, a concoction of raw fruit and vegetables. Or the tree could be a *rambutan*; my children christened the fruits 'hairy monsters' because the bright red casing of the fruit is covered in soft spikes, like a demented punk rocker's hairstyle. Inside is a delicate, juicy white flesh around a large

126

'Hairy monsters': Rambutan, the delectable fruit.

stone. It is one of the numerous local fruits, all of differing taste, that are best likened, for the uninitiated, to a lychee. There is for example the wonderfully named *kaca mata*, cat's eyes, because the stone is dark and shiny like a cat's eye. I was fortunate enough at one time to live in a house with a garden suitably fitted out with banana, coconut, mango and papaya trees and one shade tree growing next to a clump of turmeric. But the real joy of the house was provided by the neighbours' garden, which boasted two very fine *rambutan* trees, for my special enjoyment. There is an etiquette to tree planting in Malaysia. Plant a tree and it will spread; if its boughs hang over your neighbour's garden, and hence drops its leaves in their compound creating yard work, then, in compensation, the neighbour is entitled to harvest the fruit that grows on those errant boughs. I did so, to much relished effect. The point is that with the arrival and rapid growth of all the fruits and flowers, including the ubiquitous

127

bougainvillaea and hibiscus, the national flower known locally as *bunga raya*, before long a naked, bare human incursion will soon become a proper tropical scene. The individual efforts of householders will be aided by civic operations of planting roadside trees and another glorious enclave will have been added to a garden city.

Even condominiums are not immune. Menarah Indahh's covered parking area, I remember, was being delightfully overgrown. You looked down to see how bougainvillaea was being trained to spread a protective layer across the roof. The balconies of apartment blocks testify to human habitation in potted plants of all variety. No sooner had I moved into Menarah Indahh than I was despatched to Sungei Buloh to undergo the proper home occupier's initiation in plant acquisition. Sungei Buloh, then out in the *hulu*, the jungle, had been the site of the local leper hospital. The hospital closed long ago, but many of its residents remained to engage in economic enterprise; they run nurseries and supply all the other plant nurseries around the city. It is still an ideal place to visit for a swift overview of local flora. Properly instructed, I went to the source, to learn that out of misery can come the most resplendent beauty at the cheapest prices anywhere in KL. Here were shrubs and flowering plants of every shade and type, from the potted greenery varieties, like mother-in-law's tongue and all types of aspidistra, or the common palm in a pot, to delicate orchids and everything in every colour, shape and size between. Being a foreigner, on my first visit I was sternly told by my helpful local assistant merely to indicate my preferences and then remove myself while earnest negotiations about price were conducted. I am ashamed to say that for a few pounds dozens of plants were acquired, all in their glazed pots with accompanying pot trays to catch the water and prevent the soil oozing out of the bottom, an entire balcony and large window box load. By this rite of passage I had become one with my new environment and its customary laws.

Now Sungei Buloh and its plant nurseries are virtually inside the city. Successive waves of new suburban developments link it to the heart of KL. There are now so many new enclaves that cement and tiles seem to be winning out over the battle of reintegration. Many of these new developments have minuscule driveways and virtually no gardens, making one despair that time will make any difference. The pot plants are there, a banana tree sprouts in an improbable, almost impossible internecine bit of ground but there just does not seem to be the space for real character to make its appearance. In Malaysia, real character is provided by the trees. If real character is a moot point, one yet to be proved, individuality does not take long to make itself evident. The developers' strict regimen of uniformity will almost immediately give way to amendments: new rooms, covered-over balconies, different fittings and many more idiosyncratic additions witness the spontaneous divergence of human existence. The diversity and individuality on common themes multiplies exponentially. The ingenuity of local individuality cannot disguise the fact there is an increasing dissonance in the pattern books of new urban development. New houses have hardly any space to string a washing line, let alone plant a garden, and no place for a wet kitchen, a feature of all older houses. There is at most 8 degrees of diurnal difference in the temperature in Malaysia all year round. Every day the weather report, an almost religious feature of the television news, tells the same tale: 32 –26. This code means the highest daytime temperature will be 32° C, a steamy 90-odd °F, and this will plunge to a pleasant or stifling 26° C – that's the high 70s °F – in the chilly hours of the night. It can vary a degree or two either way, the highs normally ranging from 30 to 34, but that's the weather, folks, or rather the climate. However, the same degrees of temperature can feel totally different depending on cloud cover and humidity that temper the intensity of the sunshine, and according to whether there is or is not any breeze to create movement in the air. Cooking in an enclosed space is a blistering, breathtaking – literally – exercise. The answer is to cook outside, which means not only that smoke and fumes from the cooking dissipate, but the cook gets the benefit of whatever breeze is available. Hence the wet kitchen, a covered but open area outside the house. In the wet kitchen, fish, a basic ingredient of any respectable Malaysian meal, can be cleaned and washed without the mess and smells being trapped as they would be in an enclosed space inside the house. The advantages and ingenuity of the wet kitchen are numerous. They do not extend to local developers' dreams, however. On newly built estates you see how human ingenuity seeks to overcome the architect's cultural blind spot and provide what cost-cutting bulk merchandising of designer living has neglected. The simple truth is that newly built, designed-for-profit housing is about as environmentally mismatched as it can possibly be. The Malay house, the original wooden variety, was insulated, thanks to its being constructed of wood, perched on stilts to trap cool air under the floorboards, and generously supplied with slatted windows to allow the free circulation of air within. The 'modern' houses springing up everywhere in and around KL are habitable only with artificial cooling, energy-guzzling, electricity-bill inflating, room-by-room-acquired air-conditioning or, to my tastes, the infinitely preferable, and more economical, ceiling fan. Air-conditioning means windows must remain closed so that artificially generated humidity can combat the ubiquitous naturally occurring variety.

As 'modern' development has progressed, new arcane trades have burgeoned; contractors will instantly remodel to cater for what the architect either did not know or neglected to provide in consonance with local living habits, like the hand basin in the dining room. Malays eat with their hands and immediately before and after eating, therefore, seek to wash their hands. If Malays have occupied a house there will always be a basic, elegantly built-in or really elaborate hand basin in the dining room, with the necessary plumbing tacked on. Malaysian proclivities mean that not only is the city always undergoing rebuilding, so are the individual houses, often stripped down to their bare bones to be rebuilt in new, fashionable, palatial style. Even the most modest one-storey house in an undistinguished neighbourhood can go through this process of transformation.

You drive, unsuspecting, down some side street and there standing forth, glistening with white paint under a new blue tile roof, is what was once a little shoe box but is now a mini-mansion. It will be decked out with ornamental wrought iron grilles on all its doors and windows, new rooms will have been tacked on to the structure and, the final touch, a set of wrought iron, remotely controlled electronic gates have been installed that would not disgrace Buckingham Palace. However, it is the number and make of the cars in the drive, which will have been covered over to make a carport, that attest to the true status of the occupants.

Buildings in Kuala Lumpur are not mute; they are declarative statements on status and much else. Before the arrival of the Petronas 'Twin Towers', the tallest building in the world, and Menara KL, the 'communication tower', the Tabang Hajji

'Deceptively contradictory, a jumble of paradoxes': the Tabang Hajji building in the days when it used to dominate the KL skyline.

building dominated the Kuala Lumpur skyline. From a distance, it looks like an oversized concave lens with 'Allah', calligraphed in Arabic, pasted on top. Even generous souls would not consider it to be a great building, but once you get closer to Jalan Tun Razak, it does begin to display a certain engaging charm. The building has an open, colonnaded circular base, which gives it an eerie, dreamy feel. Five arches support the colonnade around the building. These symbolize the five pillars of Islam: declaration of faith in the Unity of God and the messengership of Muhammad; prayers five times a day; fasting in the month of Ramadan; payment of the poor due or *zakat*; and, at least once in a lifetime, pilgrimage to Mecca, the *hajj*. When you stand underneath the building, it seems to be suspended in air, held in place by some unspecified miracle. The moment one enters, it transforms into the structured authoritarianism one associates with the communist architecture of Eastern Europe. The Tabang Hajji building is nothing if not eclectic. Deceptively contradictory, it is a jumble of paradoxes: open and airy yet quite phallic, innovative but quite conventional in its creativity, symbolic but not profound. It tries very hard to acknowledge the Islamic history of which it is a product but is clearly quite out of sync with tradition; it is 'authentic' in a half-hearted, self-mocking tone – an apt metaphor for Malay society.

Like the Tabang Hajji building, the Malays wear their Islam around their necks, and Malay identity is just as problematic and contradictory. To be Malay is to be, by definition, a Muslim. 'Malayness' rests on three arches referred to locally as *agama, bahasa dan rajah*, literally religion/Islam, language/Malay and royalty/sultans. These foundational principles were written into the constitution of postcolonial Malaysia. So Malays cannot but be Muslims. Outsiders – Indians, Chinese, Europeans – who wish to marry a Malay have to convert to Islam and are then assimilated in the Malay community, a process popularly called *masuk Melayu* or 'becoming a Malay'. The children are classified as Malays. Therefore, the ethnic/racial category is neither purely ethnic nor racial, but ultimately a religious category. It also means Malayness synthesizes the idea of nationalism based on language and feudalism based on royalty with Islam, which is unequivocally against nationalism and feudalism. Malay Islam leans heavily towards a mystical spirituality that draws its sustenance from myths, miracles and magic. But the Malay personality, like the Tabang Hajji building, is perfectly at home with all such contradictions.

Malay Islam is often described as 'gentle', moderate and eclectic, like the Malays themselves. What this means is that Malays are outwardly quite devout, internally very superstitious and collectively heavily into mysticism. The moderation comes from the fact that Malay Islam has absorbed and embraced, due to the society's long multicultural makeup, a great deal of history and tradition from Hinduism and Buddhism, not least a constellation of Indian myths. It is, therefore, a Muslim society that instinctively demonstrates the best of the Qur'an's own ethic of multiculturalism. When Islam spread throughout the archipelago in the fourteenth century, the Malay States retained almost wholesale their existing political and social structures, which owed a great deal to earlier Indian influence, in their version of Islam. The concept of the Divine King was modified slightly and the king became 'God's shadow on earth' but the 'just and benevolent' shadows remained almost as sacrosanct as the displaced deities. The rulers and the aristocrats continued to occupy positions of absolute privilege at the top of the pyramid, while the *rakyat* – the people – remained at the bottom. The Hindu priestly Brahmin class was replaced by two new classes: the *ulama* or the religious scholars, and a new select, social class of mainly Arab folks who claimed to be the direct descendants of the Prophet Muhammad, the 'Sayyids'. The latter were seen as possessing exemplary piety and religious merit – despite evidence to the contrary – and accorded a status equivalent to royalty. The rulers, the aristocrats and the Sayyids all acknowledged the fundamental Islamic notion of 'equality before God' but insisted on social hierarchy among men. The intrinsic connection between Malay Islam and Hinduism is demonstrated by the sheer number

Masjid Kampung Laut, the oldest mosque in Malaysia.

of Sanskrit terms that have been transformed to denote Islamic concepts and practices: so religion becomes *agama*, fasting becomes *puasa*, hell becomes *neraka*, and heaven becomes *syurga*. All of these terms have mystical connotations in Hinduism; and this is a particularly strong feature of Malay Islam. There is a second mystical layer of Malay Islam; and this comes from Sufism. The spread of Islam in the archipelago coincided with a resurgence of Islamic mysticism in the Middle East. The fall of the Baghdad Caliphate in the thirteenth century led to a strong movement against the arid legalism of orthodox Islam and a consequent upsurge of Sufism. The Sufis preached a syncretic mix of Islamic dogma, neo-platonic gnosis and communal spirituality, and were more than tolerant towards pre-Islamic beliefs. Their willingness to preserve continuity with the past enabled the Sufis to make deep inroads in the archipelago and carve an indelible presence on the Malay mind.

Quite how one explains Malay Islam tells as much about the orientation of the describer as about Malay religious ideas. There is more tolerance, gentleness and humane guidance in the Qur'an than Muslim society generally demonstrates, which is saying quite a lot if you take an impartial look at its record in history. What is good about Malay society can as legitimately be ascribed to Islamic inspiration as it can to pre-Islamic survivals. On the other hand, all that is good and benign about Malay Islam does not detract from many a node of stiff-necked formalism or ardent mystification at which many a Muslim, or anyone else, might cavil. The sociology of religion looks at things only in terms of 'whatever was first is most significant', as if anything after the beginning is somehow tainted and vaguely 'inauthentic' and by such chopped logic somehow misses the essence of religious experience as experienced by the religious. Whatever footprints of influence and relics can be traced, the simple truth is Malays have for centuries sought and continue to seek their validation, explanation, interpretation and resolution within the framework of Islamic ideas.

This is not a straightforward process, any more than it is for any Muslim society, compounded as they all are from different histories, cultural bases and influences. What Islam should be, pure and untainted, is a perennial debate, when it is not a heated fractious argument, among all Muslims. Further, many Muslims are unsure that Islam means or intends them to stand or begin from ground zero, instituting religion in a vacuum, unengaged with human history and culture. Every variant of Islamic reformism finds a home in Malaysia, as does every variety of Sufism, some even verging on cult status. The brand of what is journalistically termed 'fundamentalism' is found in the east coast Malaysian state of Kelantan where it operates on the pattern book of untainted, puritanical Islam created by removing specifically Malay culture from Islamic orthodoxy. So they banned the *Mat Jong*, a Malay dance drama, because both men and women participated and male dancers would take female roles. But if culture, in so many of its guises, is 'unIslamic' to an unacceptable degree, then no Muslim society anywhere could lay claim to being truly Islamic. The path of 'fundamental' reform becomes ever more narrowly reductive, a matter of removing everything that creates not only diversity but also meaning in a particular Muslim society. This reductive process, say certain 'fundamental' reformers, must also be applied to aspects of modernity, also intrinsically deemed 'unIslamic'. They end up emphasizing a very limited number of principles (themselves heavily influenced by culturally biased historical interpretation) while loudly proclaiming the expansive capabilities of Islamic principles to create an entire way of life, the meaning of the term that Islam uses to describes itself, *din*. In practice, such 'fundamental' reform most overtly resembles exactly what it glorifies, a return to the past, in all the nostalgic simplicity Muslims invest in that idea. Living in a present past and unwilling to relinquish all those 'unIslamic' new-fangled goodies, however, can result in making a society even more dependent on all those outside forces they denounce, which can hardly have been the intention or, to my mind, the meaning of Islam. Bent on reduction, such a 'fundamental' approach comes up short on construction, creativity and home-grown solutions, which, in my book, are the true meaning and intention of Islam. Malay certainty about identity, rooted as it is in Islam, includes, involves and lives with all the contradictions, paradoxes and earnest debate that form the contemporary state of Muslims everywhere; all attempts at questions and answers are evident and available.

Given that to be Malay is to be Muslim, how the unresolved conundrums are answered is a serious matter in Malaysia. Side by side with Malay mysticism, there exists Malay formalism. The gentle and eclectic mingles seamlessly with formal punctilious orthodoxy and precise organization; appearing to be correct, observing the rules, is a major concern for Malays, a shared cultural predisposition and preoccupation. Religious education for young Malays is highly organized, a visible presence. One consequence of this education system is that Malaysia produces some of the finest Qur'an readers in the world, all with flawless classical Arabic pronunciation. But what constitutes religious education is a tradition-bound, prescribed matter, not a full-blown education in the modern sense. Malaysia, characteristically, has been in the forefront of experimenting with 'Islamizing' its modern, Western-modelled, secular education curriculum. Totalitarian secularists quail at the very thought, just as they do at the debate about values in education in all Western societies.

During the late 1980s, I was involved with the efforts being made to reform the education curriculum; this involved considerable debate on the what and how of 'Islamization'. I attended numerous conferences organized by the Curriculum Development Department of the Ministry of Education. The hope, enthusiasm and delight of these conferences were provided by the civil servants and educators. Malaysian education is a national institution, the large sums spent on education being one of the great achievements and the bedrock of Malaysian development efforts. The ministry staff are of all races and creeds, yet all of them accepted and welcomed the idea that Islam had something positive to say about ethics in education, without feeling threatened or pressurized. In itself this is a considerable feat that probably only Malaysia could manage. The discussion on Islamization, many explained, enabled them to get a better idea of the central principles of Islamic belief, and hence a better understanding of their Malay neighbours. There was a uniform acceptance that values had a place in education, for the good of society in general, for each individual in particular and for the contribution it could and should make to critical reasoning rather than blind acceptance of received wisdom, whatever its source. The discussion went a lot further. Many non-Muslims admitted they found the concept a compelling example, not merely an exercise they had to entertain by dint of the Muslim majority's preoccupations. They felt a desire to see the application of such initiatives within their own religious and cultural tradition. Religions live in Malaysia. There is evidence to suggest that, when the religious are not building redoubts against the onslaught of secularism, a common basis of mutual acceptance can enable interfaith dialogue. More importantly, this interfaith accommodation can become a natural currency of multicultural existence where it is most important, in the interactions of normal life rather than in worthy conferring among the great and the good that deals mostly with platitudes. However, it is a lot easier to enunciate the idea of Islamization than to translate it into practical textbooks and classroom practice. An uneasy tension still exists between the dominance of conventional disciplines of Western knowledge, the concerns of traditional Islamic education and the still unresolved synthesis that strives to build a new convention from the best of both. Yet, as a rapidly developing society Malaysia has gone a lot further, with a lot less brandishing of slogans and rhetoric, to integrate and translate Islamic ideas into the means for meeting the needs and patterns of contemporary life. There are Islamic banks and an Islamic University; one of the most successful developments has been the mutual funds, the Amanah Saham, which no longer cater exclusively to Muslims. Rigid formalism, mysticism, eclecticism and pragmatism: it all makes a very Malaysian mix.

One of the most notable characteristics of Malay mysticism is its emphasis on miracles; an approach to religion also promoted by the *Sejarah Malayu*. This interest, indeed obsession, with miracles is a reflection, as the Malay sociologist Shaharuddin Maaruf has noted, 'of a very worldly and sensual philosophy of life'. But the Malays do not demand any old miracles. Since the quest for miracles is essentially a desire for belief in the necessity of spiritual life, the miracles have to be firmly outside the boundaries of rationality and material signs, areas Islam rules firmly within the boundaries of routine normality. So dreams often play an integral part in these miracles. Indeed, as we learn from *Sejarah Malayu*, Islam itself came to the archipelago thanks to a dream in which Rajah Kechil Besar saw the Prophet Muhammad. If dreams shape reality, then it should not be surprising if reality imitates dreams and miracles. The narrative of Rajah Kechil's conversion to Islam actually follows the Prophet Muhammad's experience of revelation. Just as the Prophet Muhammad, even though he cannot 'read', is able to recite the Qur'an with the help of the Archangel Gabriel, so Rajah Kechil is able to recite the articles of faith in Arabic even though he has no knowledge of the language. Just as Islam is central to Malay identity, so dreams and miracles are an essential part of the Malay psychology. Not surprisingly, *karamat* (miracle) worship is a central tenet of traditional Malay Islam.

Despite its unarguably gentle and open nature, and the moderation of Malay Islam, authoritarianism runs deep in Malay society. Indeed, it starts with *Sejarah Malayu* which legitimizes the feudal social order. In sharp contrast to all varieties of Sufism, which present the world as a mere illusion, and worldly possessions as fleeting, unnecessary and an impediment to true spiritual development, *Sejarah Malayu* heaps unqualified praise on wealth, grandeur, power and military might. Not surprisingly, Malay feudalism is obsessed with absolute power, and total domination is an intrinsic value in its psychology. The Malay peasantry has always seen the conditions of its existence as an *a priori* given: the forms of the feudal structure and its hierarchy, divinely sanctioned through the agency of the rulers, determine both their individuality and their history. The people exist in a network of patronage. This is not an uncommon pattern in agricultural societies. It has advantages: ideally the hands of the ruler and aristocrats should be open, dispersing resources as well as maintaining peace, justice and prosperity among the people in a fair and equitable fashion. But then all systems, ideally stated, are, well, ideal. No system actually comes right out and says that what we offer is a benign or indeed malign confidence trick. In the past the *rakyat* had the means to subvert the system when it became too grossly abusive. They could vote with their feet, literally pick up their house and move to open up a new village outside the effective control of too obviously overbearing a ruler. In the rise and fall and interplay of power rivalries between the old sultanates of the archipelago, the doings of the *rakyat* are an unrecorded story, but they were a possible factor in the decline of some at the expense of others.

Patronage is a feature of every system of power, every human institution; patronage itself has a history, transmuting with the change in society. Look for example at the history of the mafia, the feudal patronage system par excellence. It began in peasant

Sicily and southern Italy as a means of doing what peasant, feudal societies do, enabling people to get on as best they could and get as much liberality and advancement as their feudal leaders could provide. The point about patronage, as opposed to faceless bureaucracy, is that it works by recognizing people as particular individuals with all the peculiar twists and turns of their individual and familial life and history. Where patronage is concerned individuals matter, rather than laying down rules and regulations that somehow never have the flexibility to cope with special cases, when everyone is a special case. So, in old Italy the patron, the don, was one who manhandled the far-off government and its incomprehensible rules on behalf of the peasant client. When scions of this system migrated to the United States they took their attitudes and readiness to accept patronage with them, to much publicized effect. The new dons among them were those who most effectively manipulated the system in this new and foreign field, which provided a fertile territory for robber barons. Lured by the possibilities of ill-gotten riches, the whole mafia system at home and abroad turned malignant, went rabid and enforced its criminality by old codes of 'honour' and their concomitant naked brutality. Feudal patronage under the tutelage of colonialism also underwent subtle alterations. Under the incomprehensible newness of culturally obtuse, knowledgeably ignorant colonial rulers, patronage had whole new areas to flourish and further enmesh the mass of the population in the dependent bonds of patron–client relations.

Out of a history that has shaped it, made it serviceable and offered it more ample scope than is sensible, patronage, in contemporary Malaysia, continues to be a main organizing principle of society. Kuala Lumpur as the focal point of the nation is the hub of all patronage, a city ordered, organized and visibly displaying the dispensations of patronage. Patronage concentrates power and influence in the hands of the governing class, the ruling classes as well as the newly emerging business elites who shape and mould the lives of ordinary people. In their turn, working-class Malays are largely resigned to fatalism. They manipulate the system as much as they can for their own advantage. The trouble is that modern society offers no realistic possibilities for literally picking up your house and moving off to open up a new frontier. Modern society is total – its rule runs everywhere, the major distinction it has over its precursors. On every level of society, hierarchy and social status are emphasized and a person's superiority or inferiority is, consequently, a pertinent, if invisible and undeclared, factor in any situation. The authoritarian ethics promoted by *Sejarah Malayu* takes its toll in Malay society through the interplay of arbitrary power and abject submissiveness before it. The Malays thus have an absolute reverence for power; and the ruling elite an equally extreme lack of self-restraint. The feudal psychology does not value either moderation or humility. What it does value is loyalty: total, unquestioned, absolute loyalty. The hallmark of Malay character – traditional, modern, postmodern – is loyalty to the system and those who maintain and manage it.

The Tabang Hajji building is a reflection of the deep loyalty Malays have for Islam. However, as is typical of Malaysia, more than symbolism is involved. It is not only the most clamorous Islamic building in Kuala Lumpur – it was built to house the most creative and reliable economic institution in the country. Tabang Hajji, as the name suggests, is 'the hajj fund' set up specially to help the rural Malays perform the pilgrimage to Mecca. When first established, by an Act of Parliament in 1962, it was a specific response to a particularly Malay problem. The highly religious rural Malays, ever keen to perform the *hajj*, were trapped in a poverty cycle. A villager would work and save for years, and if theft or a natural calamity did not destroy his savings, he would eventually acquire some property. When he decided to go on the *hajj*; he would without hesitation or economic consideration sell his property even if this meant selling at a loss. On his return he would find himself without land or property facing a life of destitution. In the past there was a sense of finality associated with the performance of the *hajj*, it was not only the completion of one's religious duties but also, in a sense, of one's life. There was a measure of realism in this attitude. The pilgrimage was a long and hazardous undertaking. The seminal disaster in Conrad's *Lord Jim* is the supposed sinking of a ship carrying pilgrims on their way from this part of the world to Mecca. To die on the way to or in the holy places is seen as a special blessing. To return is to have gained much in religious merit, and is denoted by the honorific Hajji or Hajjah incorporated in people's names.

In the days of aeroplanes and package tours and the best-organized system of pilgrim management in the world, old habits, the attitudes acquired from older realities, still persist. Today, when they decide to go on *hajj* Malays, in true formal punctiliousness, prepare thoroughly. They attend classes to learn about the rituals that make up the pilgrimage and obtain a proper spiritual formation for a major rite of life passage. They travel in organized groups, provided with guides. In the often chaotic throng of over two million pilgrims from all over the world, the Malaysians will be notable for the smooth efficiency with which they are negotiated through all the salient elements of the *hajj*, which extends over a ten-day period. Before departure from Malaysia the pilgrims make courtesy calls on everyone they know, taking formal leave of everyone, literally as if they may never return. It is not just the potential hazards of travel, ancient or modern, that makes them so mindful. The *hajj* also has its hazards, as was demonstrated some years ago when even the superbly organized Malays were nevertheless fatally trapped when fire engulfed a tunnel connecting one area of the *hajj* to another. When a wall collapsed under the press of humanity another year there were concerned reports in the Malaysian news media as desperate inquiries were made to discover if the Malay delegation was involved; thankfully they had already left the site before the accident occurred. To overcome the social dilemmas affecting rural Malays, Tabang Hajji was developed by Ungku Abdul Aziz, a former vice-chancellor of the University of Malaya in Kuala Lumpur, as a savings infrastructure for would-be pilgrims. The idea was to make the farmers save gradually in advance for the *hajj*. This way, they would not only benefit from advance planning, but also gain from returns on their investment and, most importantly, avoid a situation in which property would be sold at a low price due to urgent and immediate need. Tabang Hajji is now one of the most successful funds in Malaysia: it not only provides a valuable service for the pilgrims, who are no longer predominantly rural farmers; in addition, as the savers have changed, so the institution has acquired much wider economic interests and importance. It has ensured that all Malays can go on pilgrimage and, as with economically empowered Muslims everywhere, many do so repeatedly. The collective funds they devote to the purpose have become a major institution of the KLSE, the stock exchange, 'a player' in the most modern aspects of a rapidly developing economy. A conscious attempt to produce an indigenous institution designed to meet local needs and mark a sharp break from the colonial past has straddled the transition; it services and is at home in a 'miracle' economy.

II

Colonial history is not easily transcended. But what the colonial architecture of Kuala Lumpur does not tell us is that the imperial power did not always have its own way. Some intended brides are just too unwilling to be subdued. The Malay sultans, not totally immune to a little bit of imperialism themselves, have had many bitter experiences with extremely desirable but unwilling and wilful potential brides. When Sultan Mahmud's wife died he wanted a truly extraordinary new wife, someone like the wondrous princess living on the Gunung Ledang, a mountain in the state of Johore. So he sent his most distinguished court nobles up the mountain. Things became rather difficult; only one nobleman, exhausted and wind-blown, reached the mountain top, to find a beautiful garden where

143

birds sang ceaselessly and the flowers whispered poetry to each other. But in the middle of the garden there was a pavilion of human bones with a roof of human hair. In the pavilion sat a stately old lady surrounded by young girls. The old lady asked the nobleman, Tun Mahmut, why he had come. He told her. 'I serve the princess of Gunung Ledang', she said; 'I will convey the sultan's wish to my mistress.' The lady and her servants disappeared and returned a short while later. 'The princess is willing to marry the sultan', she told Tun Mahmut. 'But there is a condition. As dowry, he must provide a gold bridge and a silver bridge from Malacca to Gunung Ledang, seven dishes of mosquito livers, seven dishes of louse livers, a large flask filled with tears, a large flask of juice from young betel nuts, a bowl of the sultan's blood and a bowl of his sons' blood.' Tun Mahmut returned to the sultan and told him of the princess's demands. The sultan thought for a moment. 'Even if I give her everything else', he said, 'I can't give her my sons' blood.' And he abandoned all idea of marrying the princess of Gunung Ledang.

When the Japanese invaded Malaya, the day after they bombed Pearl Harbor, the British thought Malaya demanded too much of a dowry: defending the peninsula against an army that knew how to fight in the jungle would be like getting a flask of juice from young betel nuts. The country was certainly as desirable as the princess of Gunung Ledang but not worth several bowls of British blood. The Japanese attacked from the north and within a couple of months, they had hacked their way through the jungles to Singapore, passing Kuala Lumpur en route. Where it did not collapse, the British army withdrew; the British fleets were sunk at sea by Japanese air attacks. On 15 February 1942, the British surrendered and Malaya came under Japanese occupation.

The myth of the superior 'white man' evaporated as fast as had the British military presence in Malaya, about as quickly as the remnants of a rainstorm when the sun comes out. The Japanese played various segments of the population against each other, promoting nationalist and racial feeling. The Indians

144

were set to work on the Burma railway line and encouraged to fight against the Raj in India. The Malays were persuaded to form a Japanese version of the nationalist movement, the 'Avengers of the Motherland'. Chinese nationalism, however, presented a different problem. The Chinese feared and hated the Japanese for their brutalities in China. In Malaya, the Japanese continued in the same vein, brutally persecuting the Chinese at every opportunity. The Malayan Communist Party (MCP) took advantage of the feelings against the Japanese to recruit many Chinese into the Malayan People's Anti-Japanese Army (MPAJA). As by this time the police force consisted mostly of Malays, any clashes between the police and the MPAJA inevitably included and increased racial tension.

The Japanese left as rapidly as they had arrived. And the British returned; but they returned to a radically changed Malaya where nationalism and anti-colonial feelings were high. Gone was the daughter of Nara Diraja who could be easily abducted. The British had to contend with the princess of Gunung Ledang who was not going to be readily subdued. In exchange for depriving Malaya of its economic wealth – the rubber boom had generated profits that made it a latex Klondike – and turning its inhabitants into subject people, the British were supposed to protect the communities in Malaya. Yet the protection they offered was evident in their hasty surrender. The Japanese also contributed to this loss of confidence in the British. They were, of course, Asians who had scared off and defeated a colonial army. They had stressed Asian co-operation and the idea of 'co-prosperity', and then contrasted the poverty of the region with the wealth of Europe. Malaysians retain an ambivalent attitude to the Japanese. Their 'Look East' policy and the importance of Japanese investment in their economic growth are not without echoes of the rhetoric of their erstwhile occupiers – how often money works its magic more effectively than armies and guns, the neo-imperialist reality of the industrial complex. Yet recently, in celebration of its anniversary, the Malaysian national airline, MAS, produced one of those seminal television advertisements that give such a revealing insight into the Malay psyche and outlook. It began with three children playing with a toy aeroplane; they watch as Japanese fighter planes pass overhead. 'I remember when we had to look up to people by looking down', ran the commentary as a family of Malays made the customary bow to Japanese soldiers. The Chinese boy and his family are loaded into a truck to be relocated to who knows where. As the truck heads off, the Malay boy gives his friend the toy aeroplane as a keepsake. The Indian boy is also marched off with his family. The advertisement was a rare public reference to Japanese occupation and its subtle subtext was how the three boys, a Malay, an Indian and a Chinese, who shared a common bond of childhood friendship, were torn apart and propelled into different life choices and opportunities by their wartime experience. The advertisement shifts scene to a modern airport: up an escalator comes a middle-aged Chinese businessman bearing before him a toy aeroplane; waiting to greet him are two greying middle-aged men, a Malay and an Indian. Development has reunited the three friends, validating their common childhood bonds. It is just so Malaysian in the Malay way, sentimental, but with a genuine emotional lump in its throat, idealistic, even idealized, yet authentically tapping a real history and honestly implying how differently it impacted on different groups. Difference is important to Malaysians; their multiculturalism works through respecting significant divergence, which raises sensitive issues. Common experience and common bonds include different sensitivities, memories and mutual contention; that is why, in the end, in the Malaysian way, they can be hidden, manipulated, fought over, paraded, made evident and resolved, and still be sensitive, demanding subtlety. The correct demeanour in such circumstances is emotion, the balm of raw sentiment.

The British returned to a more politically aware nation, and a nation that expected a certain amount of contrition from the British. But remorse was never an emotion associated with the British Empire. Far from being contrite, the British actually attempted to turn the Malay States into a *colony* instead of restoring their previous status of *protectorates*. The new colony was to be the 'Malayan Union'. At the time when the jewel in the imperial crown, India, for the safety of which they had abandoned Malaya to the Japanese, was rapidly moving towards independence, a Malayan constitution, under which the Malay rulers would have to surrender their jurisdiction to the British government, was drawn up. The sultans would be 'honorary' rulers and participants in a religious council that would look after Islamic affairs but that would be headed by a British representative. The plans for the Malayan Union were as shameful and hastily drawn as the British surrender to the Japanese. The announcement of the union was made in the Houses of Parliament in London by the secretary of state for the colonies on 10 October 1945. Two days later, Sir Harold MacMichael, a special envoy of the British government, arrived at Port Swettenham (now Port Klang) to obtain the signatures of the Malay rulers. The British did not intend to give the people of Malaya much time to think about the union, let alone discuss or oppose it. But oppose it they did – in large numbers. Within months, the Pan-Malayan Malay Congress was formed to 'unite the Malays into a strong articulate body in order to obtain repeal of the [Malayan] Union constitution'.

The Malay Congress was a predecessor of the United Malays National Organisation, or UMNO, which likes to think of itself as the only Malay political organization that ever existed and that single-handedly won independence. In fact Malaya had become a hotbed of political organization, sprouting numerous political parties all directed towards similar ends by various means, with differing agendas and composition. The Malay Congress was determined to thwart the British plan to institute the Malayan Union Constitution on 1 April 1946. In a move out of keeping with British representations of the Malay character, the congress asked, almost ordered, the sultans to boycott the installation of a new British governor. They were to avoid sitting on any of the councils set up by the British, and to observe

147

Tunku Abdul Rahman at the 1951 UMNO General Assembly,
after being elected President.

berkabung – seven days of official mourning, as a sign of protest.
The Malay Congress was articulating the widespread shift in
opinion towards the sultans, whose standing in Malay eyes had
altered overnight. They were criticized for betraying the people
to the colonizers in newspapers and *pantuns*, the traditional
Malay variety of ironic poetry, and told that, if they wanted to
keep their power, they had to take care of the people's welfare.
Loyalty to leaders may be the basic premise of Malay society,
but loyalty has limits, and no position however exalted is ever
without or beyond criticism. If Malays value loyalty they are
never naive about those in whom loyalty is invested. Direct
confrontation is never the Malay way; convolution is the essence,
coming at things indirectly, preserving face and the illusion of
general agreement, even undiluted support among consenting
parties, no matter how bitter the actual difference and depth of
the divide. Therefore, by way of compensation, satire is the
national art form. Retelling the latest cutting jibe, the circulation

148

of the latest pointed funny story, the more scurrilous the better, is the fabric of life in Kuala Lumpur. The tradition of the *pantun* and the *dalit*, whose ribald commentary keeps the *wayang kulit*, the shadow puppet play, contemporary, is forever honoured and alive in the precincts of the city. Loyalty, conformism and avoidance of open opposition or conflict have their natural corollaries in subversion through satire that makes public opinion a force to be reckoned with.

Events moved rapidly. Working committees came and went. The non-Malays raised objections to certain Malay demands. The Malays adjusted their demands. The British worked with UMNO, which came into being on 11 May 1946, with Dato Onn bin Jaafar as its founder president, and with the sultans but refused to endorse the recommendations made by them. New organizations and alliances were formed. Finally, the constitution of the Federation of Malaya came out in 1948. It gave due representation to the minority groups, allowed the immigrants to acquire nationality more easily and met the conflicting demands of all contesting groups. The Malay rulers and the British signed an agreement on 21 January 1948 and on the basis of this constitution the Federation of Malaya came into being on 1 February 1948. Everyone, it seemed, was happy with the new order of things. Everyone, that is, except the communists.

The beginning of the communist uprising in Malaya is often attributed to the Asian Youth Congress held in Calcutta in February 1948. This is largely true as the Calcutta congress inspired communist uprisings throughout the region – from Burma to Malaya, Indonesia and the Philippines. Within four months of the congress, the Malayan Federation declared a state of emergency that was to last for twelve years and cost thousands of lives. Always an emergency, never a war, this vicious conflict is part of the collective experience of British males of a certain age, the age when they did their national service attempting to put out the brush fires of late colonialism all over the empire. The generation of boys too young to have had a 'good war' in the 'big show', World War Two, got their common bonding in 'dirty little wars', as a later generation of Americans termed their collective trauma. Their commanders found themselves fighting against communist bands led by the very people who had been their allies and sometimes their friends during the war against the Japanese, people they had supplied and trained to become expert jungle fighters.

The Malayan Emergency was one of the first conflicts over the political fate of what were later termed 'dominoes', but Malaya was far too economically sensitive for anyone to call it a war or a domino. It was so sensitive that it became a real emergency, presaging all the issues about what would come after colonialism and how it would operate. Communal rivalry, so painstakingly diffused in the formation of the Federation, returned to the fore because the communist movement in Malaya was dominated by the Chinese and, as before, most members of the local police force were Malays. And, once again, the jungles came to play an important part in the politics of Malaya. The communists lived in the jungles, emerging only for acts of subversion and guerrilla warfare. The Chinese squatters who eked out a living in the rural hinterland were regarded as natural allies and supporters of the communists. It was not surprising that life for the Chinese became increasingly harsh. The government decided to move the squatters into fenced camps in order to control their movements, in an attempt to starve the communists out. The British, who invented the idea during the Boer War, put this same scheme into practice in many a colonial setting, where other unwilling and unruly brides rebelled against the forced marriage of colonialism. The concept was venerable indeed by the time it was adopted by the Americans in Vietnam. The programme to deny food to the communists – known as the Briggs Plan – worked; it contributed to the defeat of the communists but it had side effects. The Chinese squatters were, ironically, better off after moving from the jungles. They had better land, on which they could build houses, and had access to electricity, schools and health facilities, while for the average Malay such basic amenities were still a dream too far. Moreover, the Malays had never supported the communists. Animosity grew again, but this time from the Malays. Racial violence loomed large.

Not all Chinese were supporters of the Communist Party. This placed moderates in a difficult position – men such as Tun Tan Cheng Lock who disliked the Federation, but equally disapproved of the violence of the communists. He tried to unite the Chinese and Indian communities, but failed; but his failure lead to the success of Tun Leong Yew Koh, who is credited with forming the Malayan Chinese Association (MCA) in early 1949. This organization provided a focus for both the Malays and the Chinese: the Malays, who could now see that not all Chinese had communist sympathies, and the Chinese, who could now display a non-aggressive face to the Federation, and identify more with the British. Meanwhile, UMNO was changing too. It allowed members of other communities to hold associate membership and Dato Onn felt that UMNO could become the sole representative of all races in Malaya. Others questioned the loyalty of non-Malay groups to the Federation. Dato Onn resigned; was brought back; and resigned again, taking most of the UMNO Central Executive Committee with him.

The breakaway group formed the Independence of Malaya Party (IMP) in September 1951, chaired by Tun Tan Cheng Lock, the president of the MCA. It was a genuine multiracial party of Malayan citizens; although it was not a successful political entity it was responsible for the union between UMNO and the MCA in Selangor, the foundation of the present National Front, the Barisan Nasional. The UMNO–MCA combination fought several local elections, the first being the February 1952 election for the Kuala Lumpur municipality, which it won handsomely. The alliance was eager to fight a national election but the British, thinking the natives to be a little 'impertinent', dismissed the idea declaring that Malaya was not yet 'ready' for such a move. Posturing followed: threats of mass resignations were made a number of times and eventually led, on 13 June 1954, to UMNO–MCA boycott of all the councils of government

Merdeka! Tunku Abdul Rahman declares independence, 1957.

in Malaya. The Malayan Indian Congress (MIC) also joined the alliance, completing the Barisan that was to survive and retain control of Malaysia for decades. The British had to capitulate. In the national elections of July 1955, the UMNO–MCA–MIC alliance stood firm.

The alliance pledged to gain independence, or *Merdeka*, within four years following the elections of 1955. It also promised universal education, one national language (Malay) and to uphold the position of the rulers as constitutional heads of states. It was concerned with ending the Emergency and offered a general amnesty. The only rival to the alliance was Party Negara (National Party) which consisted largely of IMP members. The elections were totally one-sided: the alliance took 51 out of 52 seats, an electoral pattern that also survived for decades having set the expectations and political comfort zone expected by the Barisan. Immediately after the election they began to press their demand for *Merdeka*. They argued convincingly that the Emergency would end sooner if the British were to leave, because the communists would no longer have imperialism to fight against. The British at last saw the logic of the argument and set up a constitutional commission to recommend a constitution for the new state. On 27 August 1957, a constitution accepted by most of the people of Malaya came into force. Independence followed four days later: 31 August 1957. After *Merdeka*, the communists lost their impetus and the Emergency disappeared. Malaya became Malaysia.

III

Independence made Kuala Lumpur the prime focus of all that happened in Malaysia. This was a new development, for the city had always been off-centre from its own national history. The British always viewed it from Singapore, the Rafflesian city on an island that became a state. When the British abandoned the Malay peninsula and Kuala Lumpur to the Japanese, the fixed gun emplacements of Singapore, part of its superb fortified infrastructure, were supposed to keep the flag flying in the toehold that ruled the whole region. It was a strategic decision that proved how wedded colonialism remained to its basic stance of knowledgeable ignorance. The ethos of Empire had made Singapore a pre-eminent centre, rather in the manner of the old Malacca sultanate, but without a hinterland, or with its hinterland in the hands of an enemy – so the city was always in danger. Singapore's guns were fixed and faced outward to the sea and global connections; they could not be used against an enemy who approached from the landward side, across the narrow and calm stretch of water between Johore and the island. No one had thought fixed guns needed to be trained on a subdued and tractable hinterland; it had always been controlled by other means. The British, like so many Malay sultans before them, learned that you overlook the hinterland at your peril.

The British have also tended to view the history of Malaysian independence from Singapore, where they had been in greatest force. Kuala Lumpur was a secondary administrative centre, Singapore the capital in a manner of speaking. The acclaimed Granada Television series *The End of Empire* provides a textbook example of how off-centre history operates. Its handling of Malaya looked at the issues and personalities exclusively from the Singaporean and hence predominantly Chinese perspective – one could be forgiven for not realizing that Malays actually existed at all, as a people or a community, except in the guise of old feudal and racially motivated sultans. So the Malay presence in the negotiations of the end of Empire is always seen as reactionary, out of sync with democratic modernity and genuine development. Singapore became an island state. In 1963 it joined a larger Federation with Malaysia and what is now called East Malaysia, the states of Sabah and Sarawak on the island of Borneo. This new Federation complicated racial politics even further. Singapore was forced to leave the Federation in 1965, with a collective sigh of relief. The removal made the racial statistics of Malaysia much more lucid. It had been argued, in hushed tones behind the hands, that Chinese were nearly as numerous as Malays, with Singapore included. With Singapore

Tunku Abdul Rahman with Lee Kuan Yew, 1963.

gone the Malays were unquestionably a democratic majority, the people of the land. They have been on an enthusiastic population explosion ever since, just to make sure it remains so. Urbanized Chinese have modern small families; Malays think six children is a nice family size. I have a Malay friend, a contemporary of mine, who has eleven children. In the joking, but serious, conversational habits of Kuala Lumpur this gives him national hero status. Malaysia and Singapore are still linked by a common umbilical cord, arising from both pre- and colonial history. They share a testy relationship, the kind of rivalry that befits siblings who have quarrelled, and Malaysia is still trying to keep the pace set by the older brother, the one who had all the advantages of more concerned parental care and tutelage. Singapore was a city on an island that has become an island city, a smart city at the cutting edge of the new millennium Information Revolution. The transformation is a lot easier to accomplish when you are the size of Manhattan Island or London and its suburbs; and when you have been a principal hub of a global empire, inheriting the infrastructure, expertise and existing connections this created. Malaysia reacquired its own hinterland and a much more complex social and economic structure as its portion.

The orbit of real Malay society is this hinterland, the world of the *rakyat*, the citizens. This is both cultural truth and constructed colonial history. It was the deliberate policy of colonialism to keep the Malays in the *kampung*, and keep the *kampung* out of economic development. The elite, the sultans and those who worked in the colonial administration were 'advised' by British Residents, who had to be obeyed. The process was designed subtly to reconstitute the elite into the kind of establishment aristocracy the British best understand, because it is their own kind. To protect the economic interests of the colonial planter economy, the vested interests of global capitalism, land – often the best – was earmarked exclusively for colonial development, leading to further marginalization of the rural Malays. Malay smallholders who tried to enter into rubber planting, for example, could be and were fined for their impertinence. The term Malay reserve land, a term that appears in the constitution of Malaysia, is a sensitive point with Malays for valid reasons. It is perhaps better understood with the mental imagery of *reservation* land, the kind of reservations where native, indigenous peoples were corralled to make way for colonial free range. The survival of the redoubt in a post-independence constitution is testimony to how pressurized, marginalized and determined to resist the Malays were, set on extracting the proper portion of the princess of Gunung Ledang's dowry from the dynamics established by colonialism.

The real locale of the Malay people is the *kampung*; the term's linguistic root means gathering. Getting together is an essential principal of Malay social life. The *kampung* effortlessly generates all the contradictions and paradoxes of the Malay character and psyche; it is the collective essence of being Malay. It is the world of the *rakyat*, the general mass of the people who are the clients of the system, whatever the system happens to be. It is in the *kampung* where everyone knows everyone else that the ethic of Islamic egalitarianism, collective engagement and mutual effort comes into its own in the Malay way. Militant egalitarianism, a term coined by an anthropologist to describe a comparable state of affairs elsewhere, neatly expresses the social reality that operates within and radiates outward from the *kampung*. Egalitarianism suggests formalism founded on everyone being the same; it includes overtones of collectivism and equitably sharing in the fruits of collective effort. The militant aspect is twofold. While maintaining the outward appearance of everyone being the same, everyone is engaged in trying to outdo their neighbours, individually to acquire the goods and symbols of higher status that egalitarianism, as an ethic and ideology, denigrates and vaguely suggests are illicit. The classic aphorism is of the man who spent all his money buying not one but two televisions and then loudly told everyone he never watched television. The *kampung* is a world where other-worldly Sufism seamlessly mingles with ardent pursuit of the goods and the symbols of earthly power and wealth and simultane-

The spirit of the *kampung* still inhabits the city: Lai Foong Moi, *Morning in the Kampung*, 1959, oil on canvas.

ously subverts that quest, as well as providing a rationale for the failure of the impossible dream. So the ethos of the *rakyat* in some sense spawns and supports its own brand of status seeking, reinforcing and validating the hierarchies of patronage whose clients they remain; it provides a vibrant antithesis to hierarchy and patronage, display of wealth, power and status while seeking to participate in it. It is acerbic in its critical stance towards all hierarchy and patronage, somehow convinced of the inevitable sinful potency of wealth and power. It is a truism of highly rational, never naive Malays that power corrupts. The militancy of individual striving notwithstanding, egalitarianism supports formalism, doing the correct, the right and expected thing, that translates into a submissive demeanour, a horror of individual initiative that singles a person out and thereby enhances conformism and conservatism, the traits that secure the presumptive perpetuity of an elite hierarchy. Confused? One should not be. The essence of the paradox can be explained in the very natural difference of attitude towards two traditional

157

kampung institutions: the *gotong-royong* and the *kerah*. *Gotong-royong* is collective self-help, co-operative work for communal purposes engaged in by mutual consent among equals. In this mode, it is the *kampung* in its self-sufficient aspect, a world entire to itself. The *kerah* is also collective work, often for communal purposes, but it was the compulsory labour sultans were able to call upon as a sort of feudal due from their followers, mutual consent not being included or indeed required. The *gotong-royong* is a peasant ethic, inherently democratic in a consultative and consensual sense; *kerah* tells you exactly where the real power resides and reinforces the fact that, no matter what trappings of collective identity and purpose may be employed, the masses remain dependent clients.

The *kampung* is also the domain of the *bomoh*, a compound of the shaman, the magician, the traditional healer and rustic Sufi. The post-independence history of Kuala Lumpur has been the translation, in a particular form, of the *kampung* into the city and the nation. Kuala Lumpur is the distillation of all the life it has drawn into itself, out of which its special essence is and has been made. Malay psyche and experience, like many of the hubs of the city, have been transformed in situ and yet retain and accommodate the old along with the new in a compound reality. The idea of all marching together in collective effort, while operating through dependent client status, is the foundation of the communal organization of Malaysian society and the political culture of UMNO administration. All the complexity, paradox and simultaneous self-contradiction of the *kampung* are now invested in contemporary KL, including the *bomoh*. The potency of spirits and magic within the compass of traditional Malay Islam is well illustrated by the *Ninety-Nine Laws* of Perak which were first compiled, according to Richard Winstedt, in the eighteenth century by a family of Sayyids. The *Laws* stated that 'Muslims must feed the district judge, the officials of the mosque, the magician and the midwife. The *muezzin* is king in the mosque and the magician is king in the house of the sick, in the rice field and in the mine.' Legislation extended to the character of the magician:

he 'must be long-headed, suave, industrious and truthful, and he must not have intrigues with women; if a person is sick, he must attend immediately'. The responsibilities also brought rewards: he was exempt from taxation and forced labour. While traditional Malay Islam legitimized the *bomoh*, he owes as much to *orang asli*, the indigenous peoples of the Malaysian jungles, as Islam. This is hardly surprising: the two cultures have lived alongside each other for millennia. The world of *orang asli* is a world of several hundred spirit beings which inhabit various places in the jungle, and which can do harm or good, depending upon their nature. Disgruntled spirits can cause a bad harvest, or personal illness; really disgruntled spirits can cause bigger problems, such as an epidemic of disease, or major social disorder. The worldviews of the *orang asli* and Malay Islam

Not *The Night of the Living Dead*, but a textbook image of a Malay *hantu*.

A *bomoh* heading a procession with a 'spirit boat'.

come together in the belief in *semangat*, or 'soul substance'. *Semangat* can be disturbed by supernatural forces such as *hantu*, malevolent spirits, or witchcraft, or physical factors such as food or behaviour. The *bomoh* determines the cause(s) of disturbance in the *semangat* of his patients by performing various rituals, interpreting the results and suggesting cures. The typical *bomoh* (if there is such a thing) is an expert on local plant life, minerals and animal behaviour. He will also be able to set bones, massage sprains and assist with dislocations. But his main role is to coax malevolent spirits away from their 'victims'; and he does this by a range of cures from exorcism (which may or may not involve the use of the Qur'an) to forms of role-playing (involving several people, not just the patient). The *bomoh* usually visits his patients at night, and in the first instance, tries to cure the patient by dispensing the aspirin equivalent of indigenous medicine: chants and incantation. If the patient does not improve, we move to the antibiotic stage: *berjamu hantu*, or offerings; the spirits and demons have to be gratified so that they do not feel the need to disturb the patient. In really drastic situations, when illness or a poor harvest afflicts the whole village, a spirit boat is constructed. The boat is filled with up to a hundred figures representing various spirits of the land and sea. Elaborate ceremonies involving the whole village precede the main event – that of sending the boat (and the village's malaise along with it) into the sea.

City dwellers are supposed to regard *bomohs* either with suspicion (if they are orthodox Muslims) or with disdain (if they are Westernized), yet they retain and have internalized the worldview of the *bomoh*. The citizens of Kuala Lumpur, whether Malay, Chinese or Indian, consult the *bomohs* quite regularly. Kuala Lumpur is a city of tales which are manufactured daily by a rumour mill that seems to exist nowhere yet is everywhere. Every dawn brings fresh rumours – the king has died in the night, this or that minister has run off with a Chinese/Eurasian woman, there is a run on a rather profitable bank – which circulate around the city, rise to the level of fact and then disappear with the setting sun. Many of these rumours are as fantastic as the tales of *hantu*; and they are believed with just as much conviction as the exorcisms of the *bomohs*. It is not rumour, exactly. It is a sophisticated operation of *kampung* gossip, a real social weapon for expressing criticism and putting ethics into play as an inhibiting force, by mobilizing the weight of publicly believed opinion. It is a cautionary force that attempts to constrain the powerful, keep them mindful that there are limits beyond which no sensible person should go in flagrant abuse of decency. It is a rumour mill whose metier is satire; it is always bitingly humorous, pithily observant; it works because it incorporates large grains of truth and probability embedded in what turn out to be fantastical tales. In these fantastical realms of the modern city, new breeds of *bomoh* have adapted themselves to the rapidly changing nature of Malay society. There are the *bomohs* consulted by party officials and upwardly aspiring businessmen, not for exorcism in the old sense, but a more proactive kind of exorcising of the constraints to advancement and the accumulation of wealth and power. The existence of the transmuted *bomoh* became evident in the most sensational murder trial in KL's history. Mona Affandi was a female *bomoh* with, according to repute and the rumour mill, an illustrious clientele of movers and shakers. She was convicted of murdering one of her clients, a member of parliament, in circumstances that suggest the *bomohs* too are seeking their share of wealth and profit by lethal pragmatism as well as magical means. The case was front-page, banner-headline news. As the *Ninety-Nine Laws* of Perak suggest, there is an ethical frame of expectation and validation for the operation of a traditional *bomoh*, whose purpose is to bring healing and health, physical and spiritual, to an individual and a community. The rumour mill perennially emphasizes the moral that power corrupts; it was shocked but not surprised therefore that where one should look for health and healing turned out to be exactly where one encountered abuse, corruption and the fatal flaw. Magic and miracles are not immune to disease; indeed they can become the disease itself.

The successful exorcism of British colonialism did little to fulfil
the hopes of ordinary Malaysians. The departing British left a
not-so-departing legacy: a new regime that not only continued
the development patterns of the colonial administrators but
also shared its biases and prejudices. Malaysia continued to be
an extraction economy, providing raw materials for the industries of global capital. The firms which loomed large in economic life were primarily foreign-owned. The Japanese did not
invent the system of using money to exert indirect influence
greater than guns and territorial control could achieve. The
Malays, in particular, felt that they were now being subjected to
colonialism with a local face. The problem was personified by
Tunku Abdul Rahman, the first prime minister and 'Father of
Malaysia'. Despite the eulogies, veneration and respect publicly
accorded the Tunku, he was also an ambiguous figure towards
whom ambivalent feelings are appropriate. The Tunku, himself
an aristocrat as the name signifies, was educated in London
where he spent most of his time in frivolities, attending parties
and drinking, missing exams and playing the football pools.
From the British perspective, the Tunku was the ideal post-
independence leader, a product of the class they had shaped
and moulded, the traditional feudal elite, and with whom they
had worked most closely. A devout liberal, the Tunku was an
ardent anti-communist and anti-socialist; his deep conservatism
assured the British that he would not neither introduce reforms
in politics nor restructure the economy. Malaysia would be an
independent nation but it would be business as usual. Moreover,
the Tunku believed in the colonial myth of the lazy native. The
Malays had become lazy, he said, because they didn't have to
work or struggle – the flora and the fauna of Malaysia provide
enough for everyone to eat. The masses may be poor and stupid,
he added, but they are happy and contented. Astonishingly, he
went on to argue that development and wealth might actually
change the rural poor – and make them unhappy and disgrun-

tled: 'My experience tells me that everybody wants to continue to live the life they have been living.'

The consequence was that Malays remained marginal to the economic heights of the national economy. The bald statistics are bald indeed. The modern economy was owned by foreign capital, British, American and European conglomerates, and local enterprise was in the hands of the Chinese. Only 3 per cent of the wealth of the nation belonged to the most populous majority community, the Malays. They still lived in the hinterland, the areas that had never been given the infrastructure of modernity like roads, schools, electricity, health care and all the other services; they existed in a state of pre-industrial poverty. Independence made little dint in this reality. Indeed, the best opportunities created by the ruling philosophy of development seemed to accrue to the Chinese community which had always been predominantly urban-based and urbanized by the containment policy of the Emergency. Once again the Malays felt cornered. It is often, erroneously, said there is only one Malay word that has made its way into the English dictionary. That word is amok. The Malay way is patience, perseverance, absorbing the slings and arrows of a state of affairs they cannot change, by which they are offended, yet have to endure. When flesh, blood and ethics can stand no more, the conventional response is *amok*, to run wild, turn violent and homicidal and hysterically vent all that accumulated frustration on some unsuspecting, but not necessarily totally innocent bystander. The crunch came in the elections of 1969, when it looked as if the Malayan Chinese Association would not hold its representation among the Chinese and would thereby weaken the entire Barisan structure. On the streets this was appalling news for the Malays. Fearful that their vital interests might pass into the influence and control of a politically stronger, as well as economically dominant, Chinese community, ordinary Malays went amok in a collective frenzy. The end product was the Kuala Lumpur racial riots of 13 May 1969, which have acquired a mythical dimension in Malaysian political lore. They are also a foundational principle of foreign journalistic lore. It is interesting that racial riots occurred in Singapore in 1964, but somehow fail to get the same media attention; they are not filed under 'what is to be said and remembered' in the annals of national pigeonholing. When Singapore recently presented its new millennium social policy there was a startlingly open discussion of the '64 race riots, introduced by no less a figure than Senior Minister (or power behind the throne) Lee Kuan Yew and echoed by Prime Minister Goh Chok Tong. Why race riots in KL are remembered while those in Singapore are of concern only to Singaporeans has a great deal to do with the response the two nations made to the crisis. In Malaysia the resignation of the Tunku was required by UMNO. Between May 1969 and February 1971, parliament was suspended and the country came under emergency rule. In this depoliticized, highly political breathing space an entire new concept of Malaysia as a nation was forged. What followed was more akin to a second independence than a simple shift in political strategy. In many ways another exorcism took place. It was an exorcism of the *hantu* of colonial legacy, in whose place a new institution, built out of authentic *semangat* was to be put. The projected outcome was a new Malaysia created out of a Malay dispensation. It was the consciously planned, formally ordered dream of a modernized, more equitable, multicultural nation. Founded on the perennial misunderstanding of the Malays in Malaysia, the off-centring of their real history and a preoccupation with the May 1969 riots, the entire edifice that emerged is most often wilfully and woefully misunderstood. Sometimes the wilful and woeful has been provided as much in Malaysia, for sectional and personal political purposes, as abroad. The race card, for example, is often introduced by innuendo in local political debate whenever a leader feels the masses need to be called to order. The formation of the new dispensation is a genuine UMNO product, forged within the party and operated by the governments they have dominated. Sensitive issues were to be settled away from public view, by the patrons of the new system, who by the new policies they introduced vastly increased the range and scope of their patronage, the whole nation becoming their clients.

The principal instrument for remaking Malaysia was the introduction of the New Economic Policy (NEP), which was designed to 'eradicate poverty among all Malaysians and to restructure Malaysian society so that the identification of race with economic function and geographical location is reduced and eventually eliminated'. In plain language it meant extending the facilities of development and real opportunities to the marginalized, still predominantly rural Malays. In honesty it was the only possible option. But it never meant just that, as the NEP itself stated, indeed as *Runku Negara*, the national ethos, devised at the same time also strove to make clear. The NEP set as its target 'the ownership and management by Malays and other indigenous people of at least 30 per cent of commercial and industrial activities in economy and employment structure at all levels of operation and management that reflects the racial composition of the nation by 1990'. The NEP created two categories of individuals: the *bumiputera* or the people of the land, not an exclusively Malay category, and the rest, the non-*bumiputera*. To achieve the targeted results, affirmative action, or what is also termed positive discrimination, was to favour the *bumiputera*. The Chinese were now restricted in many spheres, including the economic, by regulations designed to give special advantages to the Malays. Foreign companies and local Chinese business now had to compete with state capital, in a planned and programmed way; this was to be invested and used to create growth with redistribution.

Affirmative action, for various reasons, many having to do with the reluctance of those who actually created the mess to be contrite, is never popular. Affirmative action on behalf of a majority who also dominate the political structure and hence the levers of power is almost incomprehensible to foreigners, when it does not actually smack of and is not being accused of being simple racism. I remember meeting a newly arrived expatriate, at one of those expat social gatherings that are a fixture of life in Kuala Lumpur. Eager to demonstrate her interest in her new locale, she began to comment most unfavourably on all the nasty nuances she had gleaned. Advertisements in the newspapers regularly proclaim *bumiputera* discounts; the Chinese complain of being excluded from opportunities, especially university education, by quota systems. I had heard it all before. My dinner companion was expressing merely the clichés of received conventional wisdom about Malaysia. Sitting, as we were, in the garden of what had once been a colonial residence, which now housed an expatriate British family working for a foreign conglomerate earning rich profits from its investment in Malaysia, I declined to adopt the Malay way, never my way anyway. I decided to engage in a few home truths. This turned out to be a lot easier than it normally is. Malay experience of colonial history signally fails to resonate with most British people. My companion, however, turned out to be Irish; a modicum of facts and she quickly gathered the drift and began to think about things afresh. 'I never knew that', she repeatedly opined along with 'No one ever told me that.' Precisely, so few commentators do. But then the mere phrase 'planter society' has a resonance in Ireland that carries many volumes, volumes containing parallels that decode the subtleties of Malaysian history into the shape of issues people actually understand.

The NEP gradually began to change the face of Malaysia, and especially Kuala Lumpur and the Klang valley. Nationalized industries, concerted buildup of the infrastructure, investment in local industries and encouragement of foreign industrial investment on the one hand; on the other hand, the training and recruiting of personnel to provide education, health and a full range of social services across the whole nation. Deploying a mix of conventional economic strategies, Malaysia had a plan for everything. On paper these plans look unexceptional, based as they were on a concern for universal social welfare geared to redistributive equity. In practice it did not quite work that way. In 1990, when the NEP came to be reviewed, its targets had not been achieved. Malays had prospered: they now owned 23 per cent of the nation's wealth. But the strategic manoeuvres by which redistribution had become an established feature of the scene were already showing the strain. There was a Malay middle class – indeed a new middle class was emergent in all the ethnic communities. The children of the *kampung* now had jobs in industry, in factories, in government service, offices and shops. The economy had made the decisive shift: the majority of its population worked in industry, not the old primary agricultural production sector, and the largest export earners were manufactured goods in the electronic and electrical sector. The entire nation, except for the elite, was riding around in the national car, the Proton Saga. The motor industry was planned, intentionally founded on a green-field site that in three years went from virgin forest to industrial plant rolling out finished cars. Malaysia had looked east, taking careful note of how Japan and South Korea had developed; it was ever self-conscious and imitative of the development plans of Singapore.

Large parts of adopting and adapting these models made excellent, sound sense, on paper. The rumour mill in its traditional self-deprecatory salacious way was impressed but uneasy. It turned its attention to the culture of patronage through which all this effort operated. To effect the transformation into a industrializing economy the target had been to create Malay entrepreneurs. Both local and foreign businesses were required to have Malay partners providing a front. A lot of Malay businessmen emerged overnight and discovered that being an entrepreneur was easy pickings. Public funds were invested, but they were invested through and held by the corporate persona of political parties of all ethnic groups. So remaking the economy and society remade the politics. The formalism of communal accommodation became a rigid new hierarchy of patronage. The Malaysian dispensation forged by the Barisan after 1969 depended on decision making behind closed doors. There were sensitive issues; they could be alluded to, but never directly stated, in the Malay way. 'Certain quarters' became a standard term for referring to troublesome elements, to warn them that

167

the certain other quarters who ran everything were aware of their activities and were not amused. The communally based political front was not only the government but also the direct recipient of economic undertaking. The whole operation of the NEP was a collective endeavour, supposed to radiate *gotong-royong*. But communal formalism as a commercially incorporated undertaking operated with increasing overtones of the *kerah*. Real opportunities were handed out to a new breed of 'can do' businessmen, Chinese as well as Malay and even Indians. But the distribution of opportunity favoured those closest to the inner circles of government. The lifestyle and standard of living of the *rakyat* was improving, though hardcore poverty endured. There were more status symbols and upwardly mobile accoutrements for militant egalitarianism to aspire to and denigrate but the *rakyat* were still the mass of clients of the system, even if it was now their own politically elected elite that was the system. And the rumour mill had plenty of ill-concealed and well-known genuine scandals to add grist to its daily labours.

The aftermath of 1969 saw other social movements emerge to shape the Malaysian scene. There was Angkatan Belia Islam Malaysia (ABIM), or Muslim Youth Movement Malaysia, founded on 6 August 1971, and the Consumers' Association of Penang, CAP, a major hub in the national network of consumers' associations and of the international network of Third World non-governmental organizations. There were ALIRAN and Friends of the Earth (Malaysia). They championed the causes of the rural and urban poor, the fight against corruption in the business community, the fight for justice and against the rapid deterioration of the environment. The Malaysian polity seemed to be edging its way cautiously towards a new kind of complexity, a new informed self-critical capacity. The environment in which this might make a real difference, however, was constrained. Political parties used their collective money muscle to buy up the local media; newspapers and television were owned in indirect ways by the power structure itself. The infamous Societies Act made rigorous requirements for the registering, operation and regular scrutiny of the activities of all organizations. ABIM, CAP and ALIRAN were constant thorns in soft thighs of the ruling elite that governed Malaysia. But the ruling classes, joined by the NEP-created Malay capitalist class, still had a few cards up their sleeves. A new myth was created and, when combined with old tales of miracles and magic, it created a potent new trajectory.

v

The modern tale that enchanted Malaysians during the late 1980s and most of the 1990s is the story of how Malaysia became a 'developed country'. This story of transformation, a miracle tale, was not written by Malaysians. It is the invention of Western analysts, commentators and journalists. It took a long time for Malaysians to be convinced that something as fundamental as a miracle was taking place. Ascribing miracle status to the rising economic power of East Asia was neither a compliment nor a total endorsement from a Western perspective that began to worry about being swamped by the competitive challenge. The East Asian economic miracle tale grew into the 'Pacific Rim' phenomenon, heralding a new 'Pacific Century', a shift in the focus of world activity from the Atlantic-centred dispensation that had dominated the global economy for half a millennium. The constantly retold stories had deep resonance with the narratives of times past. Just as the religious outlook amongst the Malays reflects the stories of *Sejarah Malayu*, so the patterns of Malaysian economic development drew their sustenance from local tales of miracles, magicians and tiger spirits. Indeed, the economic story closely parallels the 'tiger *bomoh*' story that every Malaysian child reads at school.

Malaysian folklore is full of beast fables that sometimes have a moral ending and sometimes an open ending that listeners/readers are expected to close themselves. These tales tell of how clever mouse-deer or *kanchil* (now also the second small Malaysian

national car) easily defeated elephants and unpredictable tigers. One popular story tells how a *bomoh* farmer was transformed into a tiger. It is the tale of Tok Umai, who with his wife, Tok Manis, son Salam and daughter Itam, cleared a piece of land not too far from Kuala Lumpur, and started to farm. Slowly, a *kampung* emerged. Tok Umai cultivated vegetables, tapioca, maize and padi, and would go into the jungle to search for bamboo and rattan that he sold in the nearby market. One day Tok Umai decided to go deep into the jungle to an area well known for its rich crops of rattan. He got lost on the way, as people do in the jungle, and was forced to seek shelter for the night. Suddenly, as though by a miracle, an old man appeared from nowhere, sitting on a mound in front of him. Tok Umai was at first taken aback, then cautiously approached the old man, and asked if there was a village nearby where he could spend the night. The old man said the nearest village was too far, but that Tok Umai could spend the night in his hut. On the way to the hut, Tok Umai learned that the old man lived alone with his cattle. He turned out to be a gracious host and prepared an elaborate meal of dried meat for his guest. After the meal, the two men lay down to sleep on the bamboo floor. Just before he was about to go to sleep, Tok Umai heard the unmistakable roar of tigers. He could not contain his curiosity and took a peek from the window. The hut seemed to be surrounded by a large pack of tigers. Pointing towards the tigers, the old man asked Tok Umai whether he would like to look after his 'cattle'. Tok Umai replied that he knew nothing about rearing tigers. The old man then told Tok Umai that he could teach him the magic of controlling the tigers on one condition – he must leave the hut and go around and pat eight to ten tigers on their heads.

Now Tok Umai, himself a fledgling *bomoh*, fancied his luck. So he agreed. He gingerly went outside the hut and faced the tigers. Alerted by his scent, the tigers stood up and began to roar. But Tok Umai was able to pat the necessary number of tigers. The old man declared Tok Umai qualified to be his pupil and study the magical arts of the tiger. After three days' training, Tok Umai was ready to get back to the outside world. The old man gave him two sacks of turmeric and ordered a tiger to take Tok Umai back to his *kampung*. Tok Umai rode the tiger all the way to the edge of the jungle where the tiger dropped him off and then disappeared. He was unable to carry the two sacks of turmeric for the last leg of his journey, so he decided to keep a few pieces and throw away the rest. His worried wife greeted Tok Umai's homecoming with great relief and joy. When he presented edited highlights of his adventure in the jungle to the villagers, they looked at him in awe. A few days after his return, Tok Umai decided to plant the few pieces of turmeric he had brought with him. When he went to collect the turmeric he was startled to find that it had transformed into solid gold. He rushed to tell his wife and together they went to look for the two sacks Tok Umai had thrown at the edge of the jungle. In place of the two sacks, they found only lush, tender plants of turmeric. The two pieces of gold were enough to make Tok Umai a wealthy man. Already a *bomoh* and respected figure, he became a revered hero. And his *kampung* became well known in the region, attracting visitors and admirers, and the villagers became prosperous.

The Tok Umai story incorporates not just the Malaysian past but also points towards the future. Just as his *kampung* grew from his efforts to start a farm, so Malaysia itself emerged from the efforts of a few men (history always forgets women, even the fiercely independent Malay women). In the real world, the role of the old man was played by the market whose 'miraculous' properties were discovered by the ruling elite in the late 1980s. Nationalized industry was to be reshaped. Privatization, the Milton Friedman strictures on sound money and small government, and setting entrepreneurs free to let market forces do their thing was the ruling orthodoxy. National, publicly owned assets were privatized by means of the established system of patronage and circulated among the elite, under the catchphrase of Malaysia Inc. Political patronage, the real moving force behind the façade of the visible economy, routinely used its power to allocate shares in newly privatized concerns, along with the power to dispense contracts and economic opportunity. And all the time market prices were getting more and more pumped up, everything was rising, saving, spending, incomes, property prices; all in a magical fashion were making the miracle appear real. By 'touching' the other tigers in the region, by emulating their development patterns – encouraging foreign investment by offering cheap labour, lax legislation and pro-business policies, Malaysia was transforming itself into an economic tiger. But the main tenet of Malaysia's grand economic plan, like other newly emerged Asian tigers, was debt. Banks made preferential loans to well-connected businessmen; the middle class borrowed excessively to buy houses and condominiums they could ill afford and then rented them out to expatriates at extortionate rates. Most of the private deals went to the businessmen who were close to the ruling establishment; when their businesses failed, as many did, or had cash-flow problems, they could bank on cash-rich, state-run corporations to bail them out. Like the condition that the old man imposed on Tok Umai, the condition that the rulers imposed on the people was simple: forget political rights and respect political authority, follow the leader, do not question and do not voice your opinion. In return, they were promised the miraculous 8 to 10 per cent growth. The arrangement worked for almost a decade. But the Tok Umai story does not end with his return to the *kampung*.

Time passes. Salam and Itam each get married, and Tok Umai becomes a grandfather. Itam moves out with her husband to another *kampung*. Tok Manis dies. Tok Umai has a hut built for him near his wife's grave and lives alone, spending some time playing with and teaching his grandson, Abu, Salam's son. One day Abu notices that his grandfather has a lot of hair growing on his body. Tok Umai persuades the boy to keep this a secret. A few days later, Abu arrives to see a tiger coming out of his grandfather's hut. When the boy had recovered from the shock, he ran to his parents' house shouting, 'Help! Help! A tiger is attacking grandpa.' But when Salam and his wife reached the hut, they found no trace of Tok Umai. Salam could not work out what had happened; but he was sure that a tiger would not attack his father because of his magic – besides he was a *bomoh* who knew how to handle himself. That night Salam dreamt that his father had become a tiger, a *hantu* tiger. The tiger ordered him to grill a male goat, cook a selection of different rices, and bring the elaborate meal, along with all the villagers, on a Thursday night to the earth mound near the grave of his mother. Salam was not sure whether his father had turned into a malevolent or a virtuous tiger spirit. But he followed the instructions. The meal was carried to the mound and the whole family, as well as notable members of the *kampung*, waited for Tok Umai's arrival. As the full moon appeared just over the horizon, a tiger walked out of bushes and began to eat the meal. After finishing the meal, the tiger looked up at the gathered crowd, roared, and . . .

Like Tok Umai's *kampung*, Malaysians discovered that miracles don't last forever. The ruling elite had began to take the economic steroids of induced development – force-fed huge doses of capital investment that naturally showed up as economic growth – for granted. Reticence and self-deprecation began to give way to self-confidence that amongst the elite of the elite became a kind of arrogance. Many believed that their economic success was cultural, if not genetic. Then, four decades after the Vietnam War, a domino theory for the age of unbridled capitalism arrived in Southeast Asia with a vengeance.

Softly, through a Venomous Mist

I

First a haze began to appear. Then the horizon merged into a deeper gloom. A few weeks later, in September 1997, the Kuala Lumpur skyline disappeared. The haze turned into putrid smog so thick it was difficult to see more than a couple of feet in front of one's eyes. Airports had to be closed, school children were given an unexpected holiday, businesses were shut down. The smog now changed colour: the potent mixture of sulphur dioxide, nitrogen dioxide and ash painted the capital city with a mucky yellow opaqueness. The smell of burning was in the air and could not be avoided, never left your nostrils. Walking in the streets was hazardous. Skin and eyes itched, irritated by whatever was suspended in the murk. Even indoors breathing was difficult. When I opened the big windows each morning a thick miasma of smog seeped through the mosquito screens and stood suspended by its own weight in the room. Smoke was seeping even into climate-controlled buildings. Patients with breathing problems and allergic reactions began to crowd hospitals. In some parts of Malaysia, a state of emergency was declared. Kuala Lumpur became surreal: walking in the city centre watching people with gas masks hurrying along, rain covering the ground and the buildings with the sickly yellow of sulphur, traffic shimmering and melting away in the smog, was like walking within a Salvador Dalí painting.

The appearance of the haze, in itself, was not unusual. Not as severely as in Los Angeles, but for much the same reasons, smog became a regular short-term visitor to Kuala Lumpur. I first encountered the haze during my sojourn in Menarah Indahh in the late 1980s. It would arrive suddenly: one would wake up in the morning to see from the balcony the whole city shimmering behind a mist. Near the coastal areas, sea breezes would disperse it quite rapidly. But in Kuala Lumpur, the ring of hills surrounding the Klang valley would trap the haze, and ensure that it lingered for a few days. It was an unpleasant fact of life, but the city took it in its stride. In the early 1990s a combination of the as yet non-notorious El Niño and a huge forest fire in Kalimantan, the Indonesian part of the island of Borneo, kept the skies leaden grey for months. It took a while to realize that the clouds were not a portent of rain. Then one became aware of the smell of burning. And soon the unmistakable sense of gloom settled in, as people realized they had not seen the sun in weeks. But the next El Niño, the 1997 vintage, was a different story. The haze approached the scope of a biblical plague. The air pollution index shot up to 'hazardous and significantly harmful' levels. It was more than an oppressive sense of gloom: it was an intense, inescapable onslaught of every sense. And it was here to stay – for several months, at levels never before encountered. It was going to have long-term effects. Multinational companies offered to relocate expatriate families. And many took up the offer, wives and children first into the lifeboat of departing planes. Husbands stayed on grimly, under siege conditions, waiting to see if the ship would sink. Tourism was severely damaged. The haze became global headlines. The pictures of the eerie murk came most often from Kuala Lumpur, making everyone certain this was the centre of the problem, while the entire region was under the same contamination. This haze would radically transform the region's own understanding of itself.

For the past two decades, the haze had been blamed on poor, small-scale farmers, particularly the indigenous Iban tribes who live in Borneo's interior much as they have always lived. Open burning, that was the culprit. Traditionally, from time immemorial, farmers used slash-and-burn techniques, cutting back the undergrowth and then setting fire to it, to clear and fertilize the land for cultivation. But this time it was not going to be easy to pin the blame on the Ibans or other small farmers. An Iban friend of mine, married to a Briton and living in KL, was

incensed by the very idea. Her family, back in the long house in Sarawak, were suffering worse than anyone, and there were no cameras there to record their plight, or exonerate them. When we burn, my friend explained, it is over a limited zone and set so that it burns itself out quickly clearing only the desired area. What's more, should there be any mishap there were traditional means of summoning rain to dowse the fires. In fact, my friend was all for getting her mother to send the family's powerful rainstone over in an attempt to clear the air over KL. A short while after this we did have a burst of rain and I wondered whether Margaret had carried out her plan. The rain dissipated the smell of burning for a while but made no dent on the lead blanket of fumes still sitting high overhead. On television we saw the satellite photographs of the entire region shrouded under a huge black mass. These gave way to remote sensing satellite photographs illuminated with bright red spots; these were the hotspots, the source of the fires. They were liberally distributed on southern Sumatra and Borneo. The position of the hot spots coincided with large plantations, a good number, as we soon learned, owned by Malaysian companies and investors. It was not greedy timber merchants, but greedy would-be estate managers and owners looking at a cheap means of clearing the land for rubber or palm oil plantations or some other development scheme. What better way to get rid of

176

the forest cover, and no matter, *lah*, eventually it will rain! From the far reaches of outer space we found the culprits, and found we knew them already. The haze was an outgrowth of the fires of greed and corruption on a massive scale, a product of personal and corporate lust and stifling and authoritarian rule. It had brought the outer limits of economic lechery and autocratic governance into a complete loss of focus for us all, as we stumbled through the shroud of sickly smog. By the time it would eventually clear, some six months later, the economic and political landscape of Malaysia would have changed beyond recognition.

II

The haze was a physical presence, a tangible portent of all we had already known. The rumour mill could not have devised a story as large, as all-encompassing. This was not a phantasm that disappeared. It was the darker side of life made visible and tactile. We all wanted it to stop, but what it most evidently brought to the fore was the complex duality and ambiguity that had become the way of life for everyone. Malaysia had served its apprenticeship as an extraction colony. It had done time as a dependent nation, providing raw materials the price of which continued to drop in relation to the ever-increasing cost of the manufactured goods it needed to import. The cycle of poverty and dependence was a collective experience. The recession of the early 1980s led to a subtle shift of mood. Malaysia had retrenched, taken the unpalatable medicine and set a more lean and mean, cost-effective, productivity-enhanced course for the future. Like a phoenix rising from the ashes, Malaysia was set to take its destiny into its own hands. And change it did.

The late 1980s were a time of quickening pace. But general attitudes were slow to catch up with the official rhetorical style. People listened politely to the plans, the schemes, the latest catch phrases – 'Look East', 'Buy British Last', 'Vision 2020'. This last catchphrase, to acquire developed status by the year

2020, was to be based on the New New Economic Policy (NNEP), unveiled in 1990, that retained but modified the tenets of the older version. Qualitative transformation, that was the watchword. It was no good creating Malay directors and chairmen of the boards as decorative ornaments. No, what was needed was a competitive edge, a qualitative test that generated real entrepreneurs who would compete on a global stage. Privatization would be their opportunity, and the chosen vessel for their endeavours would be a corporatized sphere of large, multifaceted conglomerates, modelled on the Japanese SogoSocas.

The general election of 1990 was also of considerable importance. UMNO, the dominant party in the Barisan Nasional, had been in considerable disarray and by a variety of ploys had morphed into UMNO Baru, new UMNO, deregistering itself and registering as a new organization. The process had led to a split, with none other than Tunku Abdul Rahman being wheeled out to lend credence to a new Malay political party, Semangat 46, supposed to represent the real spirit of the original UMNO. Cynical academics at the universities in and around KL talked longingly of breaking the mould of Malaysian politics. They were completely unrealistic. Semangat formed an alternative alliance with the Islamic party, PAS, and the opposition Democratic Action Party (DAP), the repository of urban Chinese dissent. It was an inopportune, unholy alliance of unworkable contradictions. What wish fulfilment, the academic pipe dreams, did not take into account as they painted heady scenarios was sentiment on the street. The culture of cynicism was shared as much by popular opinion as academics. But on the street change was becoming perceptible, new opportunity had been delivered, vested interests in the status quo were more widely spread along with the inveterate sniping. And UMNO Baru had demonstrated more than enough ruthless political muscle. It was abundantly clear that it was still the only effective game in city or *kampung*. And UMNO Baru had one saving grace, which no cobbled-together alliance of improbable convenience could boast. It had an heir apparent, a prospect for the future, a promise that reform from within could be made real. Barisan secured a convincing victory, despite losing control of the east coast state of Kelantan, home state of the princely leader of the Semangat, Tunku Rezaleigh, and the stronghold of the Islamic party. The old organizational strength of UMNO, forged over four decades, had withstood the challenge and the new dispensation, the UMNO Baru format, was firmly in control. All eyes were turned to the future, the desperate drive forward.

Forward and upward everything went. Growth accelerated and fed on itself. It was as if a threshold had been crossed into the miracle domain of economic advancement. The economies of the West stagnated and recessed. The whole of East Asia experienced not a ripple of concern. New economic integration across the region was making whole new scenarios. The talk of the Pacific Rim, the sunrise economies, the Pacific Century came from economic analysts in the West, and in Asia they seemed passé, old hat even as they were being coined. In KL the mood began to shift. The rumour mill had real grist of high-level shenanigans to chomp on. The culture of patronage provided plenty to talk about. But the ethical edge began to get diluted. Increasingly, the discussion had a tone of wonder at the arrogance of the elite, as well as a distinct edge of sour grapes. The new dispensation, if it did not include everyone, certainly affected everyone. Building on the redistributive gains of the NEP a new middle class was visibly in existence. Jobs? There were so many available you could walk in off the street and be interviewed for a new one. Job-hopping became an upwardly mobile, salary-enhancing norm. The new middle class was made up of all communities; it was a genuine multiracial common experience. The preoccupation and concerns of this new multiracial middle class were middle-class issues of an international, globalized consumer nature. Everyone had more money to spend and more goods and services on which to spend them. Poverty had not been eradicated, but even hardcore poverty seemed to have moved up a notch, inched its way from destitution and set its sights on inclusion in the consumer boom.

Malaysia Boleh!: icons of contemporary Malaysia.

Rhetoric and catchphrases began to take on a new dimension. For all the flaws, with all the imperfections, people began to believe in the possibilities and assume that the headlines were correct. It was all summed up in the newest catchphrase, *Malaysia Boleh*, Malaysia can. Palaces materialized, making miracles manifest. By the time the next election rolled around, the face of Malaysia, and the face Malaysia presented to the world, was transformed. UMNO Baru scored a sweeping, mould-breaking victory of its own; the opposition was routed. Now even the urban Chinese voted UMNO and the Barisan. The joke was that UMNO, which controlled everything, would now have to organize the opposition, in order to ensure that there was one.

It was Francis Pym, the British foreign secretary in Thatcher's government, who at the very moment of sweeping electoral triumph warned of the potency of electoral tyranny, immediately becoming the ex-foreign secretary for his pains. Since independence Malaysia had known only one system of government. It had been ruled by an UMNO-dominated Barisan Nasional and now this had become a truly national alliance. Its track record was marred by scandal; its operating practices were regarded as legally suspect. The old Malay habit of never being naive about one's leaders had not evaporated. It had compounded like the economic growth rate. But all eyes were on the future, it was working, and it had a saving grace. It was there for everyone to see in the election night pictures. Two arms raised in celebration, the old and the new, the dark and the light. Surely the light was the future? Wait it out; take the dark demerits in one's stride. Look at the wonderful things that had already happened; look how far everyone had come. Whatever the imperfections they will not last forever: the light is there at the end of the tunnel. It was a siren song, and everyone listened.

Everyone was lured, because everyone was sharing if only in the smallest way in the roller coaster ride. True believers sprouted everywhere, believers in the fundamental transformation, believers in the future equipped with a new confidence and ready to swagger with national pride. *Malaysia Boleh*! People came to study a model economy. It was heady stuff, having made the grade and being able to tell others how it should be done, rather than copy other people's recipes for success. The national economic profile had it all: strong primary products; enviable agricultural possibilities; plenty of space to grow; lots of highly productive industry in the newest of the new cutting-edge sectors. There were enormous amounts of money sloshing around looking for an investment to grow on and a savings rate to die for and keep the multiplier effect multiplying. There was enviable political stability, no matter at what price. There was a quality of middle-class life that had more of the good things, was qualitatively better than developed nations could boast. The nation as a whole had genuinely come to believe that real multicultural inclusion was a positive strength. A sense of unity through difference was accepted. There was low common crime; people were safe on the streets, in their homes, though paranoid about security. There was less delinquency, and as yet no vicious generational divide. None of the forms of dissenting self-expression had a place in the Malaysian way, so Generation X was a fashion style and all counter-cultures gentle and mild consumer-supported options. The coming generation, like its parents, had consumer room to grow, unfulfilled expectations to strive for and a sense of belief in the future as a better place to sustain its optimism. Anyone with any sense would choose Malaysia for the long term, and having a foothold in the region was an essential requirement for global capital, the interests of which Malaysia was bent on serving. Thailand was a volatile mix of haves, have-nots and the military. Indonesia was vast, fragmented and openly corrupt under covert military rule and one-family government – the Suhartos. Singapore was too small and becoming too expensive, hotbed of the nouveau Asian chic that was everywhere. Hong Kong was on its way back to Chinese control. Warts-and-all Malaysia made sense; and it had the promise of political succession, that light at the end of its tunnel.

Then the haze arrived, and the climate changed. Conformism and complacency had taken up their abode compromising too much conscience. Malays by linguistic and cultural convention never talk about I; the first person singular perspective is absent from their worldview. Collective terms are the proper way of speaking in a society built around collective concepts, Malay, Chinese and Indian. So everyone talked of our myopia. Our conscience, disseminated through the rumour mill, knew exactly what had happened, why it had happened and who had done what. The trouble was not the knowing, but knowing our complicity. In all truth, whoever we were, the sharp intake of acrid breath had the bitter taste of our connivance coming home to sear our lungs. In the sickly miasma was reflected our misdeeds of omission, commission and complicit connivance. What we had tolerated we had now to ingest. When the clouds began to clear, the sun broke through on a scene set for conflict, a battle for the light against the dark forces which had commanded too much of our allegiance at too great a price. In the Malay way this was evident but not obvious; it worked indirectly behind the scenes. But there was a new sense of seriousness: the distaste we could not get out of our system as the haze dispersed. *I*, a bit part player, an extra, have presented *my* reflections on a story in which *I* was involved. I am often accused of making too much use of the old adage that when elephants fight it is the grass underneath that gets trampled. It is a wise adage. But as a blade of grass I know how little resistance we all put up before the battle of the two elephants. Miracles were abroad and left to the miraculous; all would be well in an orderly fashion and then we could liberate our conscience and do the right thing, the thing we wanted to do and to be made manifest, effortlessly and naturally in the normal course of things. The blades of grass made the field, and prepared the way for the elephants. It was a collective engagement, in the Malay way. It meant all Malaysians had to make a choice.

III

If you place Malaysian politics in its proper context, the collective gathering that is Malaysian life, then the story of the battle for the soul of Malaysia comes down to two men: Mahathir Mohamad and Anwar Ibrahim. Their careers bestride the crucial years and their political outlooks, agendas and styles define the issues and the choices that had to be made. The era began in

July 1981 when Mahathir became the fourth prime minister of Malaysia and ended with the incarceration of Anwar. The turbulent relationship between the two is an integral part of the modern history of Malaysia and the landscape of Kuala Lumpur.

Anwar's political career has often been described as 'meteoric' but this label overlooks a personal history of extraordinary courage and capabilities, a history overflowing with twists and turns. The son of a poor hospital worker from a rural village in the northwestern state of Penang, Anwar was born at Cerok Tokkan, a small village of rubber plantation workers and rice farmers. His house is said to have been without electricity and running water, but his family was well established in politics. Both his parents had joined UMNO in the early 1950s, and his father went on to become a member of parliament and a parliamentary secretary in the Ministry of Health. Anwar was sent to the Malay College in Perak, the school known as the Eton of the East, for his secondary education. Among his contemporaries were many who were to become movers and shakers in the new order. In 1967, he went to the University of Malaya where he read Malay studies. Deeply rooted in Malay culture, he would later make speeches that were such linguistic *tours de force*, they had his Malay audience perplexed. Perhaps because of his love of language and his own Malay cultural roots he was open to and interested in culture in the general sense of great ideas, and fine expression. A devout Muslim, he was a concerned activist at the time when a new international debate was being articulated, relating Islam to contemporary issues. It was also the era of international student activism, challenging the established order and articulating whole troves of issues concerning individual liberties, human rights and freedoms and protesting ancient and modern wrongs. Anwar became a student leader and, during his second year, led demonstrations against Tunku Abdul Rahman. Even as an established politician he would remember fondly his days denouncing the ills of society standing under a tree during these campus campaigns, and wonder why the contemporary generation lacked that kind of fire and

Anwar Ibrahim, then Deputy Prime Minister, in his office.

commitment. The wondering was an instinct no other Malaysian politician either understood or entertained. He was the force behind the creation, in 1971, of ABIM, the Muslim Youth Movement Malaysia. The organization's outlook on Islam was essentially Anwar's progressive take on religion and tradition in Asia. When ABIM became involved in demonstrations in the streets of Kuala Lumpur in December 1974 against peasant hunger and poverty, Anwar was at the helm. In the aftermath, he was arrested under the Internal Security Act, a draconian legacy of British rule, and spent 22 months in jail without trial. He relishes relating stories of his period in prison where he passed the time studying literature and philosophy and badgering other incarcerated students and political leaders to follow his example.

When Anwar was in prison, Mahathir was deputy prime minister. His route to the top of the Malaysian political ladder was just as tortuous. Mahathir was born in Alor Setar, the northern state of Kedah. He was brought up in a strict disciplinarian family and sent to Seberang Perak Malay School from where he went on to attend the Government English School. Known affectionately to his family and friends as Che Det, Mahathir studied medicine at the King Edward VII Medical

College at the University of Singapore. His education was interrupted by the Japanese occupation of Malaya; during this period he ran a stall and sold fruit in the Wednesday market in Alor Setar. After graduation, he worked as a medical apprentice at the Penang General Hospital and as a medical officer in Alor Setar, before setting up his own 'Maha Clinic'. He joined UMNO in 1946 and soon acquired the label 'Dr Umno'. By the time Mahathir launched himself in politics, he had acquired a reputation as a Malay chauvinist and champion of Malay nationalism. He won the local seat of Kota Setar Selatan constituency in 1964 only to lose it in the 1969 general election to an opposition candidate. The bitterness of his defeat increased his hostility towards Tunku Abdul Rahman, who considered him an extremist, and led to his expulsion from UMNO and political exile in remote Kedah. But he was brought back to the party and won the 1974 election and a seat in the Cabinet. From this point on Mahathir is the one whose political fortunes were truly meteoric. Within seven years, he had moved from the Ministry of Education to the office of deputy prime minister and settled into the official residence of the prime minister.

On becoming prime minister, Mahathir's first move was to induct Anwar into UMNO. In March 1982, amongst rumours that Anwar was about to join PAS, the opposition Islamic party, Mahathir produced what was described at the time as a 'major coup': he persuaded Anwar to join UMNO. A few months later, Anwar contested and won the seat of Permatang Pauh, in his home state of Penang, which was held by a PAS stalwart. Mahathir appointed him a minister in the prime minister's department and from there moved him swiftly through top jobs in the Ministries of Culture, Youth and Sports, Agriculture, Education and finally Finance; and topped it all by removing the popular but vacuous Gaffar Baba from the post of deputy prime minister, and replacing him with Anwar.

Anwar's alliance with Mahathir had three serious consequences for Malaysian politics. First, it domesticated Islamic dissent. ABIM, which was openly critical of the shortcomings of the government, especially on such issues as rural poverty and official corruption, was silenced. The radical Islamic movement, ever ready to criticize UMNO and the Barisan Nasional government, lost its edge and became a mainstream movement without much of an agenda. Second, Anwar's integrity and public persona undermined the opposition's attacks on the Mahathir regime and transformed Malaysia effectively into a single party state, or rather a single alliance of self-interested parties. The two consequences combined to produce the third: Mahathir was able to act against national institutions that could question his obsession with strict discipline, unbending loyalty and self-glorification and challenge his authority. Thus, during the late 1980s he was able, with relative ease, to undermine Malaysia's independent judiciary, one of the better legacies of British colonial rule, by placing it under parliamentary control. During the mid-1980s he strengthened the Official Secrets Act with an amendment ensuring that anyone convicted would be subject to a mandatory jail sentence of between one and fourteen years. He took the press in his iron grip by introducing an act that outlawed criticizing the government. Public demonstrations also became a privilege of the state: a demonstration could not be held without the government's permission and anyone found at an illegal assembly, meeting or procession could be arrested and jailed for up to a year. It was Anwar's lot to justify each repressive move and the scandals that came to characterize Mahathir's rule.

While Anwar held on to his progressive beliefs and principles, he was not entirely immune from the trappings of power. For almost a decade, he refused to accept titles and honours and insisted on being simply called 'Sudara' – or 'Brother'. But eventually he succumbed to the appellation game. He worked obsessively, but a great deal of his job required him to defend the indefensible. This took its toll: his attention span shrunk, he became irritable and began to seek escape in such area as horse riding (he fell off a horse and nearly broke his neck), speed boating (at which he is as inept as horse riding) and Western opera (despite the fact that he is tone deaf). But most of this was camouflage to hide the fact that his constant attempts to check Mahathir's excesses were seldom successful, although he did manage to keep some segments of the press relatively free. It was also a way of shrouding his real self and suppressing his natural inclination to fight corruption and protect the rural poor. Finally, it was a way of buying time; he would, he often said, show his true hand on becoming prime minister.

During the 1990s, the denizens of Kuala Lumpur were obsessed with a single, double-barrelled question. How far would Anwar go to curb Mahathir and would his actions undermine his chances of taking over from Mahathir? Despite Mahathir's repeated declaration that Anwar was his chosen successor, no one could be sure – least of all Anwar, who often joked that becoming deputy prime minister was a sure way to exit from politics, as Mahathir had ended the careers of three previous deputies. Every morning, Kuala Lumpur would wake up to a fresh rumour: Anwar and Mahathir have fallen out, Anwar has not defended the latest scandal and resigned, Mahathir has replaced Anwar . . . These rumours reverberated from deep within the consciousness of KL's citizens. Both Anwar and Mahathir had a very public life: everyone knew what they stood for and where they came from. Despite all the outward pretensions, they were like water and oil. Everyone knew that something was bound to go wrong with this unnatural mixture.

IV

Wayang kulit, the shadow puppet performance, is a traditional Malay art with a long history. In the days of old, religious authorities worried about the mesmerizing effect of the *wayang*: the puppeteers, using a series of rhythmic patterns, verbal, vocal, instrumental and physical, hypnotized the audience with their tales of warring kings and the sexual exploits of politicians. The tellers experienced what they told and induced these experiences in the spectators. The emotion is part of the tale and part of the performance. But you also have to read between the lines and see what lies behind the shadows, for the shadows never tell the full story; often they are complex metaphorical allusions. *Wayang kulit* is an apt metaphor for the political culture of the Malays. It is the stock journalistic and literary convention for describing and analysing politics and society. It is the visual introduction to Peter Weir's haunting film on Indonesia, *The Year of Living Dangerously*, and can be seen in any number of documentaries and news reports about the region. A cliché becomes

Shadow play: the classic leather *wayang kulit* puppet, the ultimate cliché of Malaysian politics.

hackneyed and overused because it retains a certain verisimilitude, a pertinent veracity. But eventually the cliché itself becomes a *wayang kulit*, a shadow of a shadow that enables salient stories that can and should be told to remain lurking in the enveloping gloom of metaphor.

Mesmeric effect and trading on emotion is a major ingredient of Mahathir's political formula. He is the master of manipulation, the miracle worker who conjures palaces out of thick polluted air. He is the master *dalit* who weaves a spell on everyone. 'You've got to give him credit': that's what even his most ardent opponents used to say, with a wry smile and a shake of the head. So successful were his performances that Mahathir was able to provide sufficient shadows to keep everyone entranced, whatever their personal and private doubts and distaste. There are large nuggets of home truths in Mahathir's anti-Western rhetoric, sufficient to earn him a reputation among radical and not-so-radical groups not only at home but throughout the Third World and the West. So behind the façade of the rhetoric, it appeared as if Malaysia were set on an independent course of self-generated development. In fact Mahathir's economic miracle has been old-style Westernized industrialization under the veneer of new age information technology. All of it has been dependent on foreign investment and foreign technology. It takes skill to be a *dalit*; it requires the ability to communicate the emotion of many characters. Mahathir is a master of the subtleties of the communal rhetoric of Malaysia. Whenever there is a problem he tweaks the communal instincts of the Malays against the Chinese, or uses the surrogate tactic of aiming barbs at Singapore or being hypersensitive about Singaporean rhetoric or deeds. He exploits the Islamic fervour especially beloved of the rural Malays to potent effect, so successfully that in the only operative multicultural nation in the world, one which can be proud of its record of humane toleration, he can summons the spectre of anti-Semitism. He can lure international capital for cyberdreams, while insisting that Malaysians and especially Malays will neither tolerate nor are ready for free access to unrestricted information. At times he seems to orchestrate the instincts of gullible children, with himself as the paternalist schoolmaster. How does he get away with this interplay of shadows?

As KL emerged from the haze, the riddle began to unravel, and instead of mesmeric spells the shallow edifice and abuse of power tore the last shred of subtlety from the performance. The façade of Mahathir's economic miracle was Malaysia Inc., the transformed face of economic activity which was built out of the efforts of a coterie of Malay entrepreneurs who commanded and managed wealthy conglomerates. Behind the façade was the real strength of the Malaysian economy, solid institutions, genuine potential, real resources and planned, purposeful endeavour, sound but not all that spectacular. There was an educated, hard-working and dedicated workforce with a definite propensity to save and invest. In the boom time it was the often-spoken-of fundamentals of the Malaysian economy, laid down well before Mahathir came to power and maturing over time, that sustained the façade. There was so much growth and opportunity that the flaws in the stucco work of the façade stuck in the crop of the rumour mill for a while and then just slipped through its digestive system. The apocalyptic gloom changed that; dark on dark created a new perspective. And the economic climate changed. Along with the climatic El Niño came the economic El Niño, and it was just as devastating.

The economic meltdown in East Asia did not begin in Kuala Lumpur; indeed, for some time it looked as if Kuala Lumpur might escape the worst. The East Asian region has been called the ring of fire, taking a cue from the geographic and climatic features that extend in a great circle around the Pacific basin, a volatile area of earthquake, cyclone and volcanic activity that swirls and bestirs the lands around this vast ocean. Malaysia knows none of it. It has no earthquakes, volcanoes nor cyclones. It is a kind and gentle land without these tectonic disturbances. When the financial system of Thailand went into collapse and the knock-on effect rippled across the region, KL heard a great deal about the fundamentals of the Malaysian economy and their strength to withstand regional turmoil. But it soon saw with piercing clarity that Malaysia Inc. was a worm-eaten corpse. It was a feudal corporation created in the inner circles of power. Great fiefdoms had been handed over to particular individuals. Large tracts of these fiefdoms had begun as public or communal property. The assets that became Renong, the conglomerate which accounted for the single largest chunk of bad debt clogging the Malaysian banking system, began as property of the old UMNO. By legerdemain, the naked use of political muscle, it was simply transferred to UMNO Baru by the independent agency, the Official Assignee, charged with resolving the complex holdings and ownership of the old and new UMNO. Once within the UMNO Baru dispensation, these assets were 'privatized' as the fief of a favourite. Classic feudalism on the medieval European model is not part of Malay tradition, except under Mahathir. The great mesmerizer was able to use his position, personal power and unsubtle manipulation of the levers of power to require the basic institutions of the state to do what he demanded. He found catchy names for these ploys and defended the procedures on grounds of greater national interest. The corporate façade was composed of the fiefdoms of 'can do' entrepreneurs. Read the books on the East Asian economic miracle and that is the justificatory explanation you will find for giving more to those few who had already gained too much. The reality is somewhat different. Renong has a corporate philosophy of being a tight ship, a disciplined, authoritarian corporation with company uniforms, clocking in times for everyone, regimentation in everything and managerial seances at regular intervals. In the boom time it grew like Topsy. When the reckoning was made it was clear there was no economic reason to its ragbag estate, the mishmash of good and bad companies held under its corporate, uniformed and regimented awning. Its productive companies had been made super-profitable by being awarded government contracts; the 'can do' entrepreneurs in effect did what they were told, and their corporate managers waited to be told what to do. For all the seeming authoritarian control, it was badly managed, inefficient and determined to make the public purse pay for its shortcomings.

Renong was not the only fiefdom created and distributed around a loyal set of cronies whose identity was Malaysian, including Malays, Chinese and Indians among whom Mahathir spread his patronage and who built his dream delusions. When the façade was exposed for all to see, one could visit the website of *freemalaysia.com* and have one's worst suspicions confirmed. In a virtual atmosphere of justice and freedom, the viewer could study blow-by-blow accounts of the corporate and financial activities of Mahathir's associates. Nothing that emerged in open discussion in cyberspace, the lusted-after domain Mahathir had wanted to make his own, was new. It had all been known before. But by the time the *freemalaysia* site made its virtual appearance, the disposition of the blades of grass had been transformed.

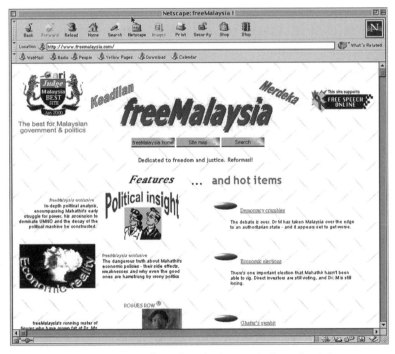

Democratizing cyberspace: *http://www.freemalaysia.com* – the freemalaysia homepage.

There is no mystery about what happened in Kuala Lumpur when the haze disappeared. The corporate irresponsibility and total lack of socially responsible corporate management became clear and unavoidable. The real battle was for control of economic management. It revealed a fundamental divide between Mahathir, who would not, at any cost, permit his façade to be swept away; and Anwar, who would not, at any cost, permit private corporate debt he considered had been irresponsibly accumulated to be bailed out by public funds. Because it was a battle for control of the economy, and control over the public interest, it had to be approached in the Malay way. Another façade had to be created to divert attention from the parasitic growth that had fed on all the good things of Malaysia's development.

In the opening months of 1998, Kuala Lumpur entered a bizarre, surreal world, in which all that was considered to be normal became abnormal, and abnormality and paranoia became the norm. The paranoia went through a number of metamorphoses. Its first form, thinking big, was now coming to a close. Everything that Mahathir did was big, very big, and was meant as much for aggrandizement as economic development. He wanted the tallest flag pole in the world (at the corner of the Merdeka Square), the longest bridge (situated in Penang), the biggest mosque in Asia (in Shah Alam, a few miles outside Kuala Lumpur), a mighty dam (in Bakun in Borneo) and the tallest building in the world (the Petronas Towers). He wanted Malaysians to climb Everest (they did) and conquer the North Pole (no one tried), and even talked of sending the first Malaysian into space. He also wanted Kuala Lumpur to become a world-class sports centre: with a Formula One circuit and a tennis championship to rival Wimbledon, and to host the Commonwealth Games – itself a dry run for making a bid for the 2008 Olympic Games. Building the facilities for these sporting showcases provided further lucrative contracts to pass to favoured companies. It was all of a piece. A justification could be made for each grand scheme individually. But collectively they were too much, too soon, and not symbols of aspiration but expressions of personal and privatized aggrandizement and folly: *folie des grandeurs*. Malaysians are supposed to be sports-mad, yet no amount of spending money on a participatory infrastructure of sporting endeavour has delivered champions or genuinely domesticated sporting excellence. The one national sport at which Malaysians are world-class, badminton, has been glutted with money and laden with financial rewards for particular successes, yet somehow this patronage has managed to deaden competitive edge and create internal bickering. Sports reporting about badminton, hockey and the notorious exploits of local football are more concerned with squabbling about rewards than the actual sport. Politics interposes itself in sport as it does in everything. The final moments of the titanic battle for the Thomas Cup, the world championship of badminton, hosted in Kuala Lumpur, stick in my memory. After each nail-biting point the television cameras cut away to the sight of Mahathir's wife, Dr Siti Hasmah, offering *doa*, a fervent prayer, for each and every point that brought victory. That was so genuinely, honestly Malay in the proper Malaysian way: the doubles team who landed the crucial victory were Chinese. Prayer, emotion, home-ground advantage and ardent national pride succeeded in defeating the old enemy, Indonesia. With the victory secure, the minister of sport spent the most time holding the trophy while he toured the country surrounded by the players. The press discussed what goodies the victors would receive. Very quickly the real sporting point, and much else, got lost in the culture of patronage that is Malaysian life and politics.

Badminton may be the shining light of Malaysian national sporting achievement but it takes second place in terms of actual sporting coverage to football, the national obsession. But when it comes to football, supporters of Manchester United and Liverpool are more numerous and ardent than supporters of the local, not nearly so proficient, football league. Television is where football lives for Malaysians, and what television delivers is a staple diet headlined by coverage of the English Premier League. When

"I LOVE NOT HAVING TO BAIT THE HOOK."

KENT
HORIZON
MAKE YOUR OWN RULES

Spot the cigarette advertisement.

corporate shenanigans put English Premier League soccer on to the highly expensive elitist satellite service provided by Rupert Murdoch's Hong Kong-based Star TV, the atmosphere of distaste and dissatisfaction was palpable. It was another instance of the feudal façade sickening the common stomach. Mahathir had made himself infamous by denouncing Rupert Murdoch and his Star TV. A New Information Order to counteract imperialism at its worst was needed, he fulminated, increasing his radical chic among non-government organizations far and wide. Colonialism and Western licentiousness were set fair to pervert and outrage Malaysian modesty, he argued for local consumption. There would be no satellite, no uncensored access to Malaysian broadcast space, he repeatedly insisted. The skies-are-closed policy lasted for years. Then Murdoch papers in Britain published a whole slew of unflattering scandals about Malaysia, coinciding with the fracas over Thatcher's aid-for-arms contracts deal with Malaysia – the Pergau Dam affair. Another round of 'Buy British Last' was instituted in retaliation. But behind the rhetorical bluster a deal was being worked out

Star TV, a free-to-air satellite broadcast network, was being lined up as a fief for another of Mahathir's favoured friends, Ananda Krishnan. He had long been known as the agent for ubiquitous cigarette advertising on television. Malaysia has a strong anti-smoking public health policy. You cannot smoke in any government building and many other public places. But the airwaves of terrestrial television channels are permanently open to cigarette brand names declaring themselves in the Malay way — indirectly. There is Alfred Dunhill, showing off *gaya, mutu, keunggelan* – style, quality and excellence – of its high-cost clothes and watches; Peter Stuyvesant whisking people off to paradise islands via its non-existent travel shop; the Benson and Hedges 'Golden Gallery', which actually opened in a space the size of a tobacco kiosk, before turning into 'Golden Bistro'. The only contribution this façade made to the anti-smoking drive was when Dunhill sponsored the local transmission of the Olympic Games. Denizens of Kuala Lumpur rose up in unison against interminable, badly timed, advertisements that made it virtually impossible to watch the games: sales of Dunhill cigarettes actually declined as smokers boycotted the brand to get what sweet revenge they could.

Now Ananda was to be handed the prize of making Malaysia a regional broadcasting hub. It was what Blackadder's Baldric would term 'a cunning plan'. Malaysia had a satellite orbiting up in space, Measat, that was not doing much. Ananda, through his company Biniarang, got the exclusive right to beam the ready-made Murdoch product down to Malaysian soil only to beam it back up to Measat, from where it would be receivable in Malaysian homes. This way the national airwaves could be a privatized national undertaking in the Mahathir way. Even in boom times, setting up the reception system was so expensive

197

for consumers that only the urban rich could afford it. The plan required people to purchase a satellite dish and decoder, and pay regular monthly fees to Biniarang's operating arm, Astro. In other words, money would be made by charging for something that was free and made elsewhere, available only because of authoritarian political control of free information, and which was financing a new local industry to generate indigenous wealth. It is an apt demonstration of the techniques of Mahathir's feudal practices. Unconscionable it might be, but you can understand why Malaysians smiled at the effrontery of it all. In this domestication process all the rhetoric about outraging modesty and New Information Orders instantly disappeared, never to be heard again. The trouble with the plan was the same as the trouble with all the other plans. It is a lot easier to deliver fiefdoms to favoured cronies than to make them genuinely competitive industries. The attempts made by Astro were inflated and delivered inadequate programming. When the going gets tough the fieflings are content to sit back and enjoy their unearned enormous profits rather than sustain the hard work, heavy lifting and home-made creative endeavour that would convert effrontery into genuine cunning. Thus the whole exercise becomes a telling testimony to naked corruption and abuse of power.

The acrid distaste KL ingested during the haze sharpened everyone's senses. Questions began to be asked and concern expressed among the professional class that freebooting free marketeering was going too far, too fast and relying too much on cronyism and corrupt practices. Malaysia was turning from an autocracy to a 'lootocracy'! It was becoming not so much a case of Malaysia Inc. as one of Malaysia plc, a private limited company, limited to Mahathir, some of his children and his chosen feudal friends. When the façade of the corporate economy began to crumble under pressure from the regional economic crisis, open criticism was for the first time directed at the entire feudal edifice. The life of the corporate sector was on the line. Its huge debts exposed its lack of real productivity. The feudal order had made paper chains of wealth, not solid products. A great deal of it was like Astro, the first to collapse into its own improbability, with chunks being quietly sold off to foreign interests, the very ones against whom the bastion of the closed-skies policy had been erected in the first place. Behind the scenes, where the rumour mill knew the blow-by-blow details, desperate efforts were being made to manipulate the financial regulatory system to ensure that the façade survived. Large-scale projects were put on hold. The Linear City, a foolish folly in a city already glutted by office and retailing developments, was supposedly abandoned. But as the crisis deepened, new stratagems had to be found. The Employees' Provident Fund, the social security and welfare savings system, the Tabang Hajji Fund and all the other funds with a single ringgit to their name were lined up ready to invest in worthless corporations and shore up their market price. The institutions were also put on alert, readied to prime the pump of the ailing economy with a new round of property development.

As routs in the local stock market continued apace, and foreign investors ran for cover elsewhere, Mahathir began a series of outbursts against the evils of a foreign conspiracy working to bring down Malaysia's success out of pure envy. He blamed George Soros – calling him 'a moron' – and the Jews, the foreign press, the IMF and the World Bank, and expressed shock at how so many of Malaysia's free market corporations had simply evaporated under the currency and stock market volatility. The markets, which had served his purpose so well, now became 'casinos'. As the recession spiralled, a generation of Malaysians who had taken for granted that their country would continue to grow endlessly at the rate of 8–10 per cent a year suddenly learnt the true meaning of poverty. Building sites remained just sites, the new monorail remained largely static and new roads remained unfinished. Dream homes were abandoned half-complete, cars were repossessed, investment in stocks of companies became worthless; as jobs evaporated, banks began hammering at the doors of the indebted, and the grocery bills shot up each time the currency lurched downwards. Every time Mahathir made a statement, the stock market recoiled. For the first time, unprecedented, virulent and open criticism of the 'Old Man' became common currency in Kuala Lumpur. 'Why doesn't he just shut up?' was the oft-heard refrain. 'Oh God, he hasn't been talking again?' was the nervous question openly asked. But throughout the economic crisis, Anwar was seen, both at home and abroad, as a safe and clean pair of hands. He blamed the crisis on corruption and lack of transparent government. His political capital escalated exponentially.

Then a curious thing happened. KL woke up one morning and learned that the prime minister was taking a two-month holiday, in the midst of the harbingers of economic meltdown, and was appointing Anwar acting prime minister. With hindsight, KL should have realized that the mice were being given the chance to play only for the cat to return hungrier than ever. At the time it looked like the most positive indication yet of a light at the end of the tunnel, and that the succession was secure. In the Old Man's absence Anwar set his face clearly against selective bailouts in the corporate sector. He introduced new and stronger anti-corruption legislation in parliament. He talked of the economic crisis as 'creative destruction', and everyone knew this was a code for stripping away the façade of Mahathir's feudal domain so that the fundamentals could breathe. The growing discontent in many sectors of Malaysian society was pushing Anwar and strengthening his resolve. The question was all about the succession, when the Old Man would not so much go on holiday as simply depart. Already, many agreed, he had stayed too long. A year earlier he could have departed with questions hanging over his head but still with honour. Had he departed any time before that it would have been with veneration and genuine gratitude. But for Mahathir, to be without office and all the power it accumulated in his hands was more than he could contemplate, despite his talk of retirement. When he returned to take up the reins, the tension in Kuala Lumpur was positively crackling. Scandal was brewing; and it had nothing to do with the real scandal of the façade economy.

Anwar is a politician with genuine charisma: he has an easy, open manner, a lively sense of humour and a real common touch. Charisma allied with his personal integrity and the stance he had taken in political life created, held and gradually expanded a loyal following around him. Malaysian politics, especially the politics of UMNO, works on the old client system. At one level it is just how things have always been and are. At another, especially during the boom years it became both benign and malignant, depending on which clients and which centres of patronage one looked at. There are always many reasons why people line up as supporters of particular politicians. In KL circles, everyone knows who is which politician's man. There have always been allegiances and factions within the overall umbrella of UMNO, which talks and presents itself as a unitary uniting structure, the liege servant of only one lord and master, the leader. UMNO's tentacles reach down to every ten households, where a party operative is responsible for mobilizing the voters and knowing their political orientation and sensitivities. This efficient grassroots organization builds up through the branch and state organizations and is topped by the delegates to the General Assembly.

In the feudal hierarchy of Mahathir's administration, the grassroots are the serfs, the General Assembly the permanent barons who make the actual decisions, the people who dispense and dispose of routine patronage to the far-flung populace. To change the face of Malaysia, to alter the terms of the UMNO dispensation, the grassroots are almost irrelevant – one has to control the General Assembly, the hardy perennial party apparatchiks. No prime minister has ascended to office without first being minister of education, because in the old days teachers were the backbone of UMNO, the most numerous Malay professional class. Mahathir changed that. The General Assembly under his administration became a way of gaining access to share allocations in privatized concerns and of being granted minor contracts. Mahathir's control over the levers of power, his ability to maintain the corporate façade, was guaranteed by his control of the patronage machine of the General Assembly. Businessmen came to dominate and, according to rumour, members of the General Assembly could be bought and sold at the leader's bidding.

The façade erected to disguise this well-known reality was the whisper campaign that Anwar was building up a hardcore faction. Anwar's men were more than clients; they were fanatic factionalists in a way never before seen in UMNO, and therefore a threat to its unity and the entire edifice of Malay solidarity. The most obvious threat they posed was to the vested self-interest of the General Assembly and the cosy patronage system to which it had grown accustomed. Anwar moved up the party echelons, people noted, not because he was beloved of the General Assembly, but because he had the backing of its lord and master, Mahathir. The economic climate changed and party members became victims of more than whispers. Through their letterboxes came poison pen letters disseminating scandal. The party, especially members of the General Assembly, were primed before the public ever had a whiff of the terms under which the battle of the soul of Malaysia would be fought. The façade of confidence in the deputy prime minister, confirmed as acting prime minister, evaporated to reveal an outright assault on his greatest political asset: his personal honour, probity and integrity. As the economy began dying on its feet, revealing all the weakness of the Mahathir dispensation, KL's attention was to be focused on a sex scandal. The publication and open sales of a book entitled *50 Reasons Why Anwar Is Unfit to Be Prime Minister* at the 1998 UMNO General Assembly had the public reeling in disbelief, for this was the wrong battle on the wrong issues. Unlike a poison pen letter, a book, whatever its contents, does not just materialize out of thin air. A Rubicon had been crossed; a real battle had been joined.

V

'Heroes who inspire Malaysian teenagers': underneath the headline in the government's mouthpiece, the *New Strait Times* (5 March 1997), young Kuala Lumpur describes the sources of its aspiration. Topping the list, way above Bruce Lee, John Lennon and 'my father', is 'Datuk Seri Dr Mahathir Mohamad' the 'caring prime minister', a 'man of great vision' who has been declared 'the Best Salesman in Malaysia'. The propaganda aspects aside, this is not an unusual choice. Mahathir incorporates all the qualities of the feudalist heroes of Malaysian tradition. He is not too far removed from such heroes as Hang Tuah and Hang Jebat, whose lives and philosophy have played a central part in shaping the modern feudal politics of Malaysia.

Every Malaysian child grows up reading *Hikayat Hang Tuah*, or rather a secondary school version of the legend. Hang Tuah, the story goes, was born in Malacca during the reign of Sultan Mansor. His father, Hang Mahmud, and mother, Dang Merdu Wati, were from a working-class background and managed a small shop. When the boy was born, his father had a dream in which Hang Tuah's head was filled with light from the moon. So, at an early stage, we have spiritual blessing for the life that the boy was going to lead. Hang Tuah became a close friend of another boy from the village, Hang Jebat, and the two boys played together and learned *silat*, the Malaysian martial arts. One day the boys, along with a few of their friends, went sailing in the open sea. As they went further and further out, they spotted some pirate boats coming in their direction. They quickly hid themselves on a nearby island but the pirates landed on the same island. There was a battle in which the pirates underestimated the young boys, who fought bravely and speared half of them to death; others withdrew wounded. On their return, the village started talking about the boys and their incident with the pirates. Hang Tuah realized that his future was to be a warrior. He persuaded Sang Andi Putra, a hermit *silat* master who lived at the foot of a mountain, to take him and Hang Jebat as his disciples. The boys trained hard and diligently with the hermit.

After their training, Hang Tuah was involved in a number of incidents, all of which enhanced his reputation as a fierce fighter. In one incident, four men ran amok, killing people on their way to the house of the city chief, Datuk Bendahara. Hang Tuah and Hang Jebat went in defence of Datuk Bendahara and killed the men. After the incident, Datuk Bendahara treated the two boys like his own sons. Later, he took the boys to Sultan Mansor, who gave each a court appointments, the title of Tun and a special *kris* with which to defend the sultan. Hang Tuah and Hang Jebat entered court service with great relish. Both, intellectually dim and with no interest other than fighting, took part in all the royal pursuits such as hunting, gambling, drinking, love-making, indulgence in pleasantries and, of course, killing. Each tried to excel the other in serving the ruler.

One of Hang Tuah's jobs at the royal court was to procure unwilling brides for the sultan. He was sent to bring the

Malay warriors *c.* 1890: the spirit of Hang Tuah and Hang Jebat.

204

daughter of the ruler of Majapahit, where he faced and killed many men. He even defeated Majapahit's most famous warrior, Tamin Sari, by playing a trick. For his achievements, Hang Tuah was given the title 'Laksamana' or 'Admiral of the Fleet'. When the sultan was ready to take a second bride, he asked Hang Tuah to kidnap Tun Teja, the daughter of the ruler of Seri Buana. Tun Teja was already betrothed to another man; and at the news of Hang Tuah's imminent arrival she was hidden at the cape of Pahang River, which was later renamed Tanjong Teja due to her stay. Hang Tuah fought for two days and, after killing Tun Teja's fiancé, brought her back to Malacca. More prestige and titles followed.

When the ruler of Majapahit, the father of the sultan's earlier wife, heard about his marriage to Tun Teja, he decided to take revenge. He sent seven men to kill Hang Tuah. Instead of killing him straight away, they decided to cause a bit of havoc in the town by stealing whatever they could find, and then went into hiding. The village started to get worried. One night Hang Tuah disguised himself as a thief and infiltrated the gang of thieves. He led them on a few successful raids; and took eight cases of gold from the palace to them. Overjoyed, the thieves decided to celebrate. Hang Tuah gave the thieves drinks that knocked them out. He then cut off their heads and brought them in a bag to show Sultan Mansor. His success won him free access to all parts of the palace.

There are a number of particularly noticeable features in the exploits of Hang Tuah. First, he is quite happy to kill anyone, in any way, without mercy or guilt. Second, he is totally, absolutely, unconditionally loyal to the ruler. Indeed, blind personal loyalty to his master motivates all his actions; it is a loyalty that supersedes ethical and moral considerations. In the narrative, Hang Tuah provides two specific demonstrations of his loyalty. His successes produce jealousies amongst other court warriors who fabricate stories about him to tell the sultan. The sultan, himself unconcerned by any notions of justice or the personal history of Hang Tuah, immediately sentences him to death. Hang Tuah reacts by declaring, 'God be praised! Tuah does not have two or three masters and he has no intention of going against his master. Make haste in carrying out the command of the honourable master.' Fortunately, Hang Tuah escapes this fate. So, a few years later, he is accused for the second time by jealous officers who suggest that he is having an affair with the ruler's favourite concubine. Once again, he is unjustly and summarily sentenced to death. Once again, he reacts with total resignation and submission: 'Tuah has no intention whatsoever to go against the master and I do not serve another . . . Total servitude is what I seek. It is best that you carry out the sentence; my life is my master's to do with as he pleases.' This time, the sultan gives Datuk Bendahara the responsibility of getting rid of Hang Tuah. He, however, believes in Hang Tuah's innocence. He takes our hero across the river to a hut, where Hang Tuah lives secretly in exile.

Hang Tuah's position at the royal court is now taken by his old friend, Hang Jebat. Hang Jebat, who is also highly trusted by the sultan and has open access to the palace, is angry about the unjust treatment of his childhood friend. He was also concerned that his own career may follow in the footsteps of Hang Tuah. So, he rebels. But what form does the rebellion take? He takes his anger out on the women in the palace: 'Hang Jebat had sex with the attendants and saw that no one dared criticize him. Then he had sex with the ruler's favourite entertainers; still no one dared to criticize him. Then Hang Jebat had sex with the ruler's favourite concubines.'

That was sex too far! But the sultan could do nothing about Hang Jebat's actions. He would kill anyone who came near him and excused himself by saying it was done to avenge the death of his best friend, Hang Tuah. Eventually, Hang Jebat drove the sultan and his men out of the palace and took control. At this point, Datuk Bendahara informs the sultan that Hang Tuah is alive and will resume his service if the sultan pardons him. The sultan promptly agrees; and we are set for a final duel between Hang Tuah and Hang Jebat.

When Hang Tuah appears before him, Hang Jebat is shocked to see him alive. But before the duel starts, Hang Jebat asks for a moment to 'clean his *kris*'. He does so by killing everyone in the palace so that 'blood dripped from the palace like rain'. But why would Hang Jebat commit such a heinous act? He offers us an explanation by telling Hang Tuah, 'my heart was enraged in knowing that you had been killed by the Bendahara, whereas you have not committed any offence . . . When a person who had served so well had been killed, why not I? I acted this way because as long as I had obtained a bad name, why not go all the way . . . to justify fully the label "rebel" and the bad name.' Then, the two former friends fight until Hang Jebat is mortally wounded. But Hang Jebat does not die immediately; he runs amok for several days during which he kills thousands more innocent people. Hang Tuah observes this with total passivity and without concern.

It is a paradox that, in an overtly Islamic society, the values exemplified by Hang Tuah, the hero, and Hang Jebat, the rebel, have permeated so deeply. They represent the kind of values that Munshi Abdullah, author of another classic of Malay literature, condemned so strongly. The people, Munshi Abdullah wrote, lived in a state of anxiety and fear of a rapacious and predatory ruling group. They kidnapped the wives and daughters of their subjects and killed anyone for the slightest excuse as though they were, to use the words of Munshi Abdullah, 'killing ants'. Court warriors like Hang Tuah and Hang Jebat were the instruments through which the rulers satisfied all their whims. The values of Hang Tuah and Hang Jebat – blind loyalty, aggression, murder and plunder of the masses – embraced so strongly by the Malay feudal elite, are totally opposed to the values of the Malay masses and the peasantry. As the Malaysian sociologist, Shaharuddin Maaruf, notes in his *Concept of a Hero in Malay Society*, Hang Tuah and Hang Jebat represent 'the counter-values' to what rural Malays have traditionally believed and worked towards. 'The Malay masses emphasized the qualities of neighbourliness, co-operation, conformity and perseverance. This conflict in the value of the ruling group and the subjugated people is a central feature in Malay feudalism, giving rise to two conflicting system of values existing side by side.'

As the champion of Malay feudalism, Mahathir identifies closely not just with Hang Tuah and Hang Jebat but also the rulers and the style of governance represented in *Hikayat Hang Tuah*. Through most of his reign, Mahathir has run Malaysia as a personal fiefdom, fulfilling his every whim and fancy. He has demanded, and with few exceptions received, total blind loyalty from his ministers and members of UMNO. In the role of Hang Tuah, he has defended Malay interests without much conscience and with determined ruthlessness. While the economy was booming, he could live with a troublesome deputy and allow him to express the counter-values of the Malay masses. Occasionally, he even welcomed the anti-corruption and pro-peasantry activities of Anwar, since they acted as a lever he could use to keep his associates in line and subservient to him. Anwar could also be used for a charm offensive on the international scene that Mahathir could never manage. But the economic crisis transformed all that and brought Hang Jebat into play. At first, Mahathir sought to represent Anwar in the Hang Jebat role – as a disloyal warrior who used his power to have illicit sex. 'Et tu, Brutus!', he said at an UMNO General Assembly. Even though homosexuality has deep roots in Malay culture, and Kuala Lumpur can be said to be the homosexual capital of Southeast Asia, rural Malays have a particular aversion to sodomy. So to discredit Anwar in the eyes of his natural constituency, he added the charge of homosexuality – a charge that also carries a prison sentence of up to sixteen years. But then he made a quick about-turn and assumed the role of Hang Jebat himself. He had to stand up to someone who was going to sell the whole country to the IMF, he declared. He relished his own representation as a rebel against the West and the international financial system. And, if you are going to be labelled as a rebel, you might as well go all the way *à la* Hang Jebat. So Mahathir ignored the interests of the people and imposed draconian rule on Malaysia. Munshi Abdullah's description of the dread and dismay of the masses living under a grasping ruling elite echoed throughout Kuala Lumpur.

VI

On 2 September 1998, after months of growing tension, Kuala Lumpur was a city on the verge of revolt. Rumours began to circulate that Anwar was about to be sacked. At the routine Cabinet meeting at which it was decided to close the Malaysian economy to the outside world by introducing strict currency exchange controls and prevent further flight of foreign investment, Mahathir presented Anwar with an ultimatum: resign or be sacked. Anwar refused to resign. In the evening, a letter of dismissal was delivered to his official residence where supporters had been gathering throughout the day. Troops of the crack Operational Forces were mobilized from their barracks on the other side of Kuala Lumpur and stationed themselves to block off the access road to Anwar's residence, located obliquely opposite and further along the same road as the prime minister's official dwelling. The following morning the newspapers were full of not the sacking but details of a court case. Various police and prison officials had made affidavits essentially repeating the allegations contained in the *50 Reasons* book and allegedly confirmed by their investigation of local businessman Dato Nallakaruppan, an occasional tennis partner of Anwar. Dato Nalla had been arrested for having a number of unlicensed bullets at his home. Instead of being charged for a misdemeanour under the Firearms Act, he was being held under the Internal Security Act and facing the death penalty. Details of the affidavits had been broadcast before they had actually become matters of public record in the court. Despite all the pressure, Dato Nalla resolutely denied all of the salacious allegations that involved Anwar, who was not a party to the lawsuit and therefore had no means to object or to

209

defend himself. The public release of the scandal was orchestrated to provide supposed justification for Anwar's sacking. The dynamic of the façade of scandal had been set: it was about moral fitness, not economic policy. That evening a meeting of UMNO's Supreme Council was held. Anwar attended for fifteen minutes; and emerged to announce that he had been expelled from the party. Later, Mahathir emerged to confirm the news and receive a barrage of eggs and vegetables. Anwar returned to his official residence to discover that the electricity and water were turned off. The deposed deputy prime minister and his family hastily packed what they could of their possessions into cars and removed to his private home. The focus of Kuala Lumpur gravitated towards that house in Bukit Damansara.

Anwar now became the centre of an extraordinary phenomenon. The city was gripped by consternation and anxiety. Fear stalked the streets, among the conspicuous presence of police and the operational forces brandishing their armour. But Anwar, supposedly dismissed in disgrace, found himself surrounded by an ever-increasing crowd. They arrived at his house at all hours of the day and night. Marquees were hastily put up in the garden and chairs set out to accommodate the overflow from the house. The visitors were a cross-section of Malaysian society: from ordinary workers to leading professionals, politicians, scholars, social activists, housewives with their young children in tow, old people, Malays, Chinese, Indians, Eurasians. They sat quietly in the garden singly, in twos and threes, or gathered in larger huddled groups. After prayers at regular intervals during the day, Anwar would emerge from the inner reaches of the house. He would make the rounds of the public rooms and the garden, shaking hands, greeting people and being consoled by the visitors, many in tears, as they talked to him. In the first two days the visitors overran the house itself, leaving Anwar his wife and six children only the upper floor as a refuge. At night, the crowds would increase exponentially in expectation of a speech.

Gradually a pattern emerged at this new political centre of activity. Public address equipment and televisions were installed under the marquee in the garden. The swelling crowds, a sea of humanity spilling out to flood the surrounding streets, would wait patiently for Anwar to appear and deliver a speech. Anwar's speeches, and those of political, academic and religious notables who turned up at the evening gatherings, were recorded on video and audio cassettes. A new cottage industry emerged overnight. Stalls appeared outside the compound selling the tapes. Thousands of videos and audiocassettes of his speeches were being sold daily. Food stalls appeared at a nearby junction to cater for the visitors who came and often stayed waiting and watching, just being there, for hours.

The atmosphere at the city's new nerve centre was a strange mixture. It seemed to cover the entire gamut of emotion. There was concern, sympathy, outrage, fear, commitment and determination and a strange kind of suppressed elation. Suddenly, things seemed that much clearer. People noticed that Anwar seemed rejuvenated, recouping the zest and fire of his time as a student activist and ABIM leader. Perhaps it was relief that his time as public defender of the indefensible was over. A women in green *baju* captured the feeling when she was heard telling Anwar, 'Ah, Dato we're back where we should be again, like the old ABIM days.'

Nobody had any illusions. To visit was to be observed, not only by those within the compound but by uniformed police stationed at the access road and probably by plain-clothes policemen who mingled with those inside and outside the compound. The sense of fear was a new experience for everyone involved. This was not the Malaysian way. The ring of fire, the overt police states, military regimes and open repression of other countries in the region were not part of the experience of Kuala Lumpur. It happened elsewhere. The Malaysian way resolved difficulties behind closed doors, giving a public face of calm and general sense of security. Now everything was exposed, in the open: the façade of scandal was paraded in the officially controlled media and public dissent owned the streets.

211

Fear did not stop the crowds swarming around Anwar. Many saw this swirling hotbed of activity as shapeless, a kind of disorganized, chaotic aimlessness. Perhaps it was. But whoever said breaking the habits of a lifetime would be easy or well organized? Cities seldom move to a higher level of consciousness in a planned and ordered way. But Kuala Lumpur realized that a break from the past had occurred. There was a single word on everyone's lip: 'unprecedented'. What had happened to Anwar was unprecedented. How the city had come out in his support was unprecedented. For many of those who arrived at Anwar's compound it was a moment of choice. They could continue to subscribe to the official worldview, or they could begin thinking for themselves – without knowing quite where the decision would take them. The decision would have consequences in terms of jobs, scholarships for their children, advancement of their careers, contracts for their businesses, all the signs and symbols of wellbeing that had become such an essential part of Kuala Lumpur life in the boom years. A truly unprecedented moment of awareness was underway. To be at Anwar's compound was for many to cross a line in the sand. What one leaves is often easier to define than the goal one is struggling towards. They came to Anwar's compound because they did not want more of the same, because they felt they had lost and gained something. They flocked to Anwar in shock because he was a lost leader. They stayed because somehow in his exile from power he offered a new kind of opportunity, a fresh start: he was a better leader. Unprecedented.

A week passed after the sacking; the initial incredulity gave way to outrage and indignation. The city acquired a collective will that was gaining strength daily; and it acquired a perception of what this collective will might be able to achieve. One can only say that this is what it felt like to mingle with the crowds, what one sensed from listening to their conversations. No one, but no one, actually believed the scandalous sexual allegations against Anwar. Initial incredulity soon gave way to outrage and indignation. Fear of impending arrest hovered over Anwar and his closest associates. His adopted brother, Sukma Dermawan, an Indonesian who had acquired Malaysian citizenship, disappeared. No one knew where he was; it was assumed he had been arrested. It was publicly announced that Anwar's staff, his press secretaries and private secretary had been sacked and would be interrogated. His former speech writer, Munawar Ahmad Anees, a Pakistani who had settled in Kuala Lumpur, was arrested in a dawn raid on his house and imprisoned in Bukit Aman, the police headquarters in Kuala Lumpur. Lawyers began to present themselves at Anwar's house to offer their services. As one of them explained, he had never been an Anwar supporter or connected to Anwar in any way. Simply, the sequence of events and statements by the prime minister, politicians and police were all too much to bear. The Malaysian legal system was being subverted.

Kuala Lumpur was hosting the Commonwealth Games, and heads of state, including Queen Elizabeth II from Britain, were about to make their way to town. When the expected arrest did not happen, Anwar decided to commence a series of visits around the country to take his case to the public. His venture outside Kuala Lumpur had been postponed a number of times due to fears for his safety. When he did leave the city, he went straight to his constituency in his native Penang. There he proclaimed the 'Permatang Puah Declaration'. It states: 'We the citizens of Malaysia of all cultural and religious backgrounds are determined to launch a movement for comprehensive reform' that would 'eradicate graft and abuse of power', 'strip the opulent and greedy clique of their power to manipulate the market' and 'sanctify the power of the people through democratic means'. It was to be a reform movement that 'champions economic justice, one that advocates fairness in economic growth and distribution so that the rich do not get richer at the expense of the poor', and 'reinforces a dynamic cultural identity, where faith in our noble cultural traditions is intact, but there is openness to all that is good in all traditions'. Reformasi, the Movement for Reform, was officially born.

The slogan began appearing on T-shirts, posters, headbands and badges, all of them available and avidly acquired by visitors to Anwar's house. The slogan of Reformasi was 'Enough Is Enough', but there was much more yet to come. The nightly gatherings at the house and the rallies in Penang spread to Alor Star, Kedah, Malacca, Trengganu and Kota Baru. In Malacca the authorities cut off the electricity supply but the crowds came nevertheless and Anwar shook hands with most of them. The speeches in different cities were more than repeat performances. They were a rising crescendo, borne along by a tide of growing public indignation. At each meeting Anwar became more outspoken and explicit in citing details of corruption. He became more implacable in his opposition to the status quo. The crowds loved him all the more for it. It was as if what had been circumscribed to the realm of private gossip and the phantasms of the rumour mill had suddenly found their proper elevation as public debate. Kuala Lumpur had not experienced this kind of public participation before.

On 17 September 1998, a Saturday, Kuala Lumpur was stunned by the news that Munawar Ahmad Anees and Sukma Dermawan, who had been held incommunicado without benefit of legal representation, had appeared in court. In two hasty summary hearings each admitted to charges of permitting themselves to be sodomized by Anwar. Those who saw the two in the court had no doubt: they had been tortured. Munawar Ahmad Anees's wife did not even recognize her husband, was physically restrained from speaking to him by the police and left the court knowing only that he had been sentenced to six months' imprisonment, but without the least idea on what charge. Each later appealed his conviction and sentence, claiming he had been forced to make a false confession. That day, Anwar gave his angriest, most impassioned and most stirring press conference. 'The entire jurisprudence of civilized countries', he said, 'rejects confessions or pleas of guilt extorted under manifestly cruel circumstances.' He added: 'The ordinary criminal law of the land, which is meant to protect the

214

innocent and punish the manifestly guilty, has been sordidly misused to achieve the evil ends of despotic conspirators.' He defied the authorities to arrest him, not pick on innocent bystanders. As always at his press conferences he sympathized with the reporters from the local media. 'I know you file these stories', he told them, leaving it understood that little he said would find its way into the Malaysian media. The following day he addressed a huge rally that stretched from the National Mosque, where he spoke, to Dataran Merdeka, the city's central square. After weeks of being baited by his accusers to swear an oath on the Qur'an to proclaim his innocence, Anwar complied. The devout Muslim is aware that the Qur'an itself cautions against taking oaths on the Holy Book. The *ulama*, the religious scholars and official embodiment of Islamic organization in Malaysia, had been far from pleased at this patently incorrect and self-serving baiting coming from UMNO politicians. Now things had changed: there were official charges laid against Anwar; the time was right to take an oath, the *ulama* declared. The impact on the assembled crowd was electric. One could not see a single dry eye. Anwar returned to his home elated by the size of the crowd who had defied all intimidation and distractions to attend the rally. An hour later, while he was in the midst of another press conference, heavily armed police wearing ski masks broke down the door of his house and arrested him. He was driven off in a van to the Bukit Aman lockup to be held under the Internal Security Act. Part of the crowd leaving Dataran Merdeka heard of the arrest and began a march on the prime minister's residence. It was an angry but peaceful crowd that included many family groups with young children – even dissent and protest are a family gathering in KL. They were met by riot troops who fired tear gas and water cannon. Throughout the night, circling helicopters could be heard overhead, to the accompaniment of police sirens and army trucks driving along the roads. The city woke up on Monday morning to witness police in riot gear on the streets, roadblocks on the highways, troops moving around the capital. Any vehicle carrying more than two or three people was being stopped and its occupants interrogated. 'These things don't happen here', people kept saying.

But 'things' kept on breaking the 'unprecedented' barrier. Immediately after his arrest, Anwar was beaten unconscious. When he eventually appeared in court there were gasps of surprise at the signs of a black eye – which later became a symbol of resistance – and seriously damaged ear. Mahathir claimed that the injuries were self-inflicted. When this claim was refuted by a doctor permitted by the court to examine him, Mahathir said Anwar must have 'provoked' the police. He went on television to describe, in lurid prose, perverse sexual acts that he claimed had been committed by Anwar. People were shocked as much by his coarse language as by his assumption that the Malaysian people would believe him. The state-controlled media launched an open season against Anwar. The inspector-general of police gave a press conference in which he visibly lost his composure and demanded that the cause of his displeasure, a representative of the foreign press, come and see him later. This telling incident was caught on camera. It was later confirmed that it was the inspector-general of police himself who had viciously beaten Anwar on the night of his arrest.

As the façade of lurid scandal was operated through the courts and the controlled media, a new joke made its rounds on the street. It was not lost on the local wags that Washington was embroiled in its own sex scandal at precisely this time. 'They've been watching way too much CNN' was the punchline as the twists and turns of revelations and evidence in court sought to parody the Lewinsky affair. If the Washington case had the infamous cocktail dress, the Kuala Lumpur one had a mattress with its own alleged telltale stains. It was brought out, and with ceremony paraded in front of cameras before being soundly demolished as having no evidential worth whatsoever. In sophisticated city circles people were openly saying: 'Even if Anwar is guilty, so what, I just don't care.' There were more than enough lurid sex scandals among the UMNO leadership,

The story that shocked the nation.

along with every other kind of venality. Nothing that was charged against Anwar or brought in evidence or rumour against him matched the publicly discussed shortcomings of his accusers and persecutors. The public wanted to be rid of a turbulent leader who offended Malaysian sensibilities and showed contempt for any opinion other than his own.

Anwar's trial was regarded by many as a kangaroo court. The court proceedings intimated, when they did not openly confirm, all that Anwar had claimed – that he was the victim of a conspiracy, politically motivated and operated at the highest levels of government. As a conspiracy it was shoddily made, arrogantly

217

executed and threadbare in content. To work, the conspiracy relied on harassing and forcing confessions from patently innocent and vulnerable individuals. The case was a façade: it convinced no one; its only purpose was to secure the inevitable conviction. When the initial charges proved lacking in credibility they were summarily changed midway through the trial to charges requiring a lower burden of proof. The conclusion was a six-year jail sentence. The significance of the sentence was not lost on anyone. It was designed to keep Anwar out of politics for the lifetime of two parliaments. Presumably by that time even Mahathir, whose officially quoted age has stuck determinedly at 73 for some years, expects to be past caring, and to have reaped all the rewards even he can desire.

The incarceration of Anwar was supposed to end the heady counter-culture of political protest. The Malaysian public had been given a few days to blow off steam. According to the rumour mill, Mahathir had been assured that public dissent would exhaust itself in ten days, hastily reassessed to ten weeks, then ten months. None of these predictions proved accurate. Under the calm of daily life a new force was abroad in Malaysian society. There are many ways to mobilize the traditional forms of compliant subversion. The facts of Anwar's beating had to be publicly acknowledged because two guards on duty when he was brought to the prison made formal affidavits of the events. It did not matter that the media was controlled and operated by UMNO, the rumour mill had discovered its moral and ethical centre and Kuala Lumpur is a city without secrets. Few Malaysians have access to the foreign media, few can afford the satellite dish that delivers CNN and CNBC news broadcasts. But what is being said in Malaysia and around the world is available through the Internet, out there in cyberspace, the domain that Mahathir had spectacularly planned to develop as a physical location just outside Kuala Lumpur. He had been working for years on his plans for a Multimedia Super Corridor centred on Cyberjaya, a new city to house new age industry. Before he could turn his dream into brick and mortar, Malaysian citizens made cyberspace a new public domain and arena of political debate. Malaysian use of the Internet became the most advanced example anywhere of the potency of this new medium to subvert authoritarian rule. Log on to the Web, enter the name Anwar Ibrahim into any search engine and you will be rewarded by lists of dozens of sites you can visit. Proceed to any of these sites and in Behasa Malaysia or English you can have all the news and debate that has no public space on Malaysian soil. A quick download and the material can be circulated among family, friends, relations and neighbours. The official *Anwaribrahim.com* website was hastily put together; and crashed almost immediately due to the vast number of people trying to log on simultaneously. More sites appeared and multiplied by mirroring themselves. The minister of education warned that computers in schools were not to be used to download material from the Internet, giving acknowledgement of the mechanics of the new dissent. Hari Raya came and went and proved to be a mass consciousness-raising exercise. Kuala Lumpur folk *balai kampung*, went to their home villages, as they always do, but stuffed in their luggage were the videos and audio cassettes of Anwar's speeches and all the latest information from the KL rumour mill. The sunrise industries Mahathir had courted were giving a new dawn to the political dissent and the public debate he sought to outlaw.

Anwar was convicted and imprisoned. One trial was not enough for the singular obsession of the Old Man. A second, equally suspect trial was arranged. Through it all, visible at each session of the court, was the new focus for dissent. A small, frail figure wearing traditional *baju kurung* and *tudung*, supported on each side by two young girls: Datin Seri Dr Wan Azizah Wan Ismail, Anwar's wife, and their two oldest daughters, Nurul Izzah and Nurul Nuha. A new social movement, Reformasi, the Reform Movement, and then a new political party, Keadilan, the National Justice Party, were formed. At the helm of both is the indefatigable Wan Azizah. It is not the first time in Asia that wives and daughters of fallen political leaders have been required to assume the mantle of leadership. Wan Azizah has emerged as the embodiment of the modern Malaysian experience. The mother of six children, she was a working wife, an eye surgeon at the government University Hospital, who has always been a mainstay and anchor of Anwar's political career. Her physical frailty belies her strength of character and steely determination. She swiftly gave ample evidence of her ability to master the steep learning curve of moving from political wife to political leader. She toured the country speaking to enthusiastic crowds numbering in tens of thousands at a time. Nurul Izzah, the oldest of the children, was a teenager with an irrepressible good humour and zest for life. She was just beginning her pre-university course when political disaster overtook the family. She returned home to become an instant political star on the Internet where her personal website attracted many young Malaysians who dreamed of a new and better future.

VII

Kuala Lumpur is visibly the same city I first came to know, a city perennially morphing itself into a new form. But something fundamental has changed. When the spell is broken, a shadow puppet play becomes a cloth screen behind which an old man waves buffalo hide cut-out figures in the dim light. Mahathir may continue to command his audience and hold the reins of power and patronage. But the ability of the master *dalit* to mesmerize is slipping. Malaysians have an inordinate ability to patiently and silently absorb insult, effrontery and mortification of their cherished values. But silence and patience are not the same as assent, and are most certainly not approval. Throughout its history Malaysia has been open to the world. To cling to power Mahathir has made a last desperate effort to close Malaysia in on itself under his iron grasp. The smog and fumes of air pollution have been replaced by an even more distasteful political haze. It may well be that behind the façade of repression another *wayang kulit* performance is in the making. It will be a collective performance, one in which Malaysians will enact all the alternate possibilities of their traditional values, the ones that have conveniently been downplayed and overlooked during the Mahathir years. The messages I receive all tell the same tale: this is not what our culture is; this is not worthy of us; this is not Islamic; this is not what Malaysia should be. I will not be returning to KL until the city has made its next transformation, when I expect it to look the same as ever and yet be profoundly different from the place I have known.

Virtual Megalopolis

The apartment building standing perched on the lip of a great earthen Kuala Lumpur is infamous for its traffic jams, caused not only by the sheer number of cars on the roads but the impatient, lane-hopping, wait-for-no-one attitude of its drivers. Malaysian drivers are the ultimate individualists: they will snake, squeeze or simply plough their way through non-existent openings only to get trapped and box in everyone else, also attempting similar manoeuvres, into one solid tangled mass. Waiting in line and taking turns would make travelling quicker for everyone. But alas! Everyone shouts at everyone else, 'Aiyo! Grandfather's Road! Alamak!', and drives straight into 'a lotta jam'. Living at Menara Indah I had plenty of time to get to know the idiosyncrasies of Malaysian road users. My lonely condo was at the very far end of Jalan Ampang, the most congested road in the city. All the time I lived there they kept building more and more condos along Jalan Ampang with a consequent increase in the number of cars seeking to use the road. But I would not have you think Jalan Ampang is the only bottleneck in town – perish the thought. Making my weary way back to Menara Indah meant negotiating many a slow crawl before one arrived at the ultimate gridlock. That is how I came to discover one of my favourite places in the city. Inching my way down Jalan Rajah Muda, I always had plenty of time to observe a line of traditional Malay houses, set back and slightly below the level of the road. Elegant and graceful, they always provided a serene counterpoint to the stressful motorized tussle. One day I was giving a friend a lift to collect a new *baju*, the Malay dress, from the tailor. This required turning off Jalan Rajah Muda and entering Kampung Baru. It was only then I learned that the few traditional Malay houses seen

A traditional Malay house: it could be anywhere in peninsular Malaysia.

from the main road were not isolated curiosities, left-over relics, but outliers of a *kampung*, a village in the city. Kuala Lumpur in its usual manner has not overwritten everything in its path, but enfolded perseverance and preservation, juxtaposition and complexity within its physical presence as well as its social being. Kampung Baru is not the only village enclave that is now part of the city, but for me it is the most delightful.

Baru means new; so Kampung Baru translates as 'New Village'. But even when it was established in the wake of Kuala Lumpur's first building boom there was nothing really new about this inner-city hamlet. It is a gathering of Malay houses as they have always gathered. The wooden houses are raised on pilings of various heights. Each house is slightly different, the general format providing much scope for variation and various ornamentation in the latticed windows, porches, front steps and gables of the pitched roofs. Once within Kampung Baru one can meander through streets and streets of these homes, some converted into stone and concrete forms as the final morph of their life history of adaptation. The traditional Malay house grows out of the soil, built from readily available materials, wonderfully adapted to the climate and environment and therefore endlessly resilient, able to accommodate the vicissitudes of life that go on within. Even in the midst of a bustling city, the houses, surrounded by fruit trees and flowering shrubs, maintain an aura of age-old quiet and contentment, even down to the occasional chicken pecking around in the yard. It is a peaceful counterpoint to 'off-stage' rumblings of the city.

City planners and property developers have had their eyes on Kampung Baru for decades. It is all out of keeping with the persona determined and devised for a cutting-edge postmodern city. And it is undoubtedly prime real estate, close to two major districts of rampant development. Do not romanticize Kampung Baru, I remember a friend telling me as I eulogized the wonder of discovering this authentic Malay jewel in the heart of the city. Living there is not as idyllic as rustic dreams would have it, I was told. Probably very true. But established communities in the heart of developing cities, places where people live and have forged their own lifestyle and human infrastructure are worth much, much more than inflated land values and the expansion of the latest in developers' dreams of sophisticated living. I was brought up in the planned redevelopment of London's East End; I know whereof I speak. I spent my teenage years working with community groups that sought to cope with the less-than-idyllic effects of the planned utopia that fast became modernized wastelands of despair, a new kind of slum environment, the slum of arrogant disposal of people without their consent or engaged involvement. A gathering of people in an environment they have made compatible with their history and its forms, whatever its shortcomings, is a bastion worth defending. That is all I know. Kampung Baru brings the old ethos of *kampung* life vibrantly alive in the heart of Kuala Lumpur. I always took visitors to see it. A visiting architect friend of mine hired a car and driver and off we went. Of course the architect oohed and aahed. What stuck in my mind was the words of the old Chinese driver, who, it turned out, was a born-and-bred Kuala Lumpur resident intimately acquainted with Kampung Baru. He spoke with enthusiasm and pride about the place, 'they may look a little rundown on the outside, but they clean as a new pin inside', he noted as he took us down side alleys and into parts I had never seen before. 'We come here for the best Malay food in town', he added as we passed a row of the inevitable hawker stalls. He had much else to say that clearly showed his appreciation that this was the heart of real Malayness pumping the lifeblood of identity into the city and the society that it makes up.

Kampung Baru has survived and resisted all the building booms that are the history of Kuala Lumpur. The first major building boom was initiated by Frank Swettenham, the third British Resident, when he took over administration of the city in 1882, a year after the great fire had destroyed most of the metropolitan area. Swettenham wanted to transform Kuala Lumpur into a city of permanent brick buildings. He was an Orientalist par excellence, having made a serious contribution to the representation of the Malays as innately lazy and pathetic. He set about transforming Kuala Lumpur into a city straight out of the *Arabian Nights*. The mad building spree that started in the mid-1890s and concluded in 1911 ended with the Moorish/Mughal architecture of the Federal Secretariat Building, Old City Hall, the General Post Office and the central mosque, Mesjid Jamek. Even today these buildings retain the Arabian Nights feel, especially at night when they are illuminated by a tracery of lights picking up their distinctive outline. And the best place to appreciate this is still from the picture windows of the main ballroom of the Selangor Club. The *pièce de résistance* was the railway station that combines the iron and glass of the Industrial Revolution with whimsical Arabian towers. Swettenham even had the British clock tower crowned with a Moorish cap. Architecture often reflects the power structure of a society; and the Moorish skyline of colonial Kuala Lumpur sings ostentatious tunes from the Orientalist hymnbooks. Kampung Baru is a statement against that past, just as it is a symbol of resistance against the consumerist present and the incubus future. The residents of

Kampung Baru have been threatened and pressurized, tempted with ultra-modern substitutes for their traditional houses, and coaxed with huge bribes and the promise of becoming instant millionaires, but they have determinedly and stubbornly refused to abandon their village. Abandonment would mean giving up a community with resilience, self-sufficiency and cultural bearings. Such notions of traditional integrity have no price.

Kuala Lumpur has been engaged in serial building booms since Swettenham's time. The immediate aftermath of *Merdeka*, independence, provoked the emergence of a spate of nationalistic buildings like the Parliament House. But the frenzy that characterized Swettenham's era was only matched in the building boom of the 1990s. The imperial vision was now replaced by 'Vision 2020', launched by Mahathir in 1991. A century apart, the two visions could hardly be more similar. Swettenham's Kuala Lumpur echoed his perception of the Malays, an amalgam of exotica and lethargy. Mahathir's vision reflects his notion of what the Malays should be. Vision 2020 is not a complex idea; indeed, it is not even a vision. Ostensibly, it means that, in the year 2020, Mahathir wants Malaysia to be a fully developed country like, and yet unlike, any other industrialized state. In reality, it is the projection of Mahathir's own designs on to Kuala Lumpur, a demonstration of his absolute power. In Mahathir's vision the Arabian Nights theme is replaced by a technodream – the city as a high-tech theme park. Despite Kuala Lumpur's Tardis-like propensities, its ability to be bigger on the inside than it appears from the outside and to continually reinvent itself Mahathir had to move outwards, stretching the city like a rubber band. Kuala Lumpur merged with PJ, Petaling Jaya, Subang Jaya (the site of the old airport) and further afield to the new town of Shah Alam, the satellite city where the national car is produced. But that wasn't enough. The city had to be stretched even further – until the rubber band snapped.

II

Rulers with delusions of absolute power have always built monuments as a testimony to their legacy. It is a sad reflection, but one worth calling to mind, that some of the greatest monuments of Muslim architecture are in fact mausoleums, houses of the dead. Mahathir was not satisfied with a monument or two – the Petronas Twin Towers or the biggest international airport in Southeast Asia, an airport so costly it has been abandoned by many international airlines, and thus caters to less traffic than its predecessor. To protect its business the national airline had to bend to the local clamour and announce that it would return some domestic routes and the shuttle service to Singapore back to the old airport. The old Subang Airport is just half an hour's drive from the centres of the city, convenient to get to for everyone. The new airport in the forest is an hour-long drive at least into the technovoid for a thirty- to forty-minute flight to Penang, Kota Bahru or Singapore. The airline's clientele made the logical choice. They just kept on driving along the major north–south highway that links the city to the airport, instead of taking the plane. The tolls on the highway are less than the airfare, and by driving they would arrive at their destination in hardly more time than it would require to hang around the airport, board a plane, fly to their destination, deplane and then get into the city. Nor was it enough to transform all of Kuala Lumpur into a city of personal homage. Like the Shah of Iran, Mahathir wanted to create Great New Cities, a string of cities, adjacent to Kuala Lumpur and connected together as a vast urban complex – a model megalopolis for Asia. It is a vision not too far removed from those of the classic villains of the Bond films: Dr No's city under the ocean, the golden city of Goldfinger, the city-within-a-city hideouts so beloved of Blofeld. Dr M, as he is known popularly, has all the necessary requirements and paraphernalia of a mad, evil megalomaniac.

With his 'Vision 2020', Mahathir drove all of Malaysia to a frenzy. Essentially a technocratic dream of hyper-modernity, the heart of the vision is the 'Multimedia Super Corridor', a 15 by 50 kilometre (9 by 30 mile) zone of high-tech electronic space south of Kuala Lumpur, designed to make the city the information hub of Southeast Asia.

As the propaganda brochure proclaims, this bigger-than-Singapore corridor is 'a gift from the Malaysian government' to the world. The 'bigger-than-Singapore' is not a random illustration but a deliberate indication of a determined rivalry, a ploy to best the erstwhile centre of colonial control. The MSC is intended to 'revolutionize how the world does business' by 'integrating ground-breaking cyber-laws and outstanding information infrastructure in an attractive physical environment'. The 'attractive physical environment' of the Super Corridor incorporates no less than three new cities and a cluster of mini-cities. Putrajaya, at the prime focus of the Corridor, is to be the new capital of Malaysia, the final off-centring of Kuala Lumpur. A model for future electronic governance, it is designed to create a 'paperless administration', complete with electronic bureaucracies – all government departments linked into one vast network – and citizens' smart cards that serve as national identity cards and double up as credit cards. So the prime minister's office, at the nucleus of this electronic utopia, would know just what every single Malaysian is up to at any given time. The crown jewel of Putrajaya is the prime minister's palace. As Anwar said in the video he made just before his arrest, Mahathir gave 'direct orders' to build 'the most beautiful and the biggest' official palace for himself. Substitute gaudy for beautiful and you have a good idea of what it looks like. Next to Putrajaya, Cyberjaya: the dedicated 'intelligent' city for multimedia companies. Cyberjaya is based on a 'teleport concept': just as the crew of *Star Trek* beam themselves up from one space–time location to another, so Cyberjaya beams Malaysia up to a brave new cyberage where it has the status of a fully developed country. It is an electronic paradise or, to put it technically, a 'World Wide Manufacturing Web'. Companies fortunate enough to be located here have real-time operational control of product design and development, manufacture and marketing, and logistics and distribution around the globe, 24 hours a day, 365 days a year, from a central location in this Brave New World. Special laws that encourage the free flow of information and protect intellectual property, and unrestricted and uncensored internet access, all of them in direct contradiction of the actual practice by both government and society in Malaysia, are supposed to provide ideal opportunities for telemarketing, technical support and technological expansion across borderless markets. The brain of Cyberjaya is the Multimedia University, which links corporations located here with a cluster of high-tech research centres beavering away to push the boundaries of information and communication technologies. Adjacent to Cyberjaya is the airport city. Occupying some 100 square kilometres (38 square miles), the new Kuala Lumpur International Airport was built not just as Asia's largest airport but also as the centre for Malaysia's emerging (or now not-so-emerging, depending on how sees it) aerospace industry. Its sophisticated electronic information network is designed to integrate seamlessly with other Multimedia Super Corridor projects, even when all that its passengers know is frayed edges.

The northern border of the Multimedia Super Corridor is marked by the Kuala Lumpur tower, Menara KL, the tallest telecommunications facility in Southeast Asia, and the Kuala Lumpur City Centre complex, the KLCC. The development provides eighteen million square feet of mixed-use space, including offices, condominiums, hotels, shopping centres, a conference and exhibition centre and entertainment centres. It is a self-contained 'intelligent' city within a city linked with dedicated fibre optic cables to the Super Corridor. However, as the more cynical inhabitants of KL point out, the only intelligent function it has performed is the starring role it had in the film *Entrapment*, with the ex-Bond actor, Sean Connery. There are a number of other half-finished mini-cities littered across the megalopolis. Sumurcity, the world's first covered city, was to be developed on 29-hectare site – 'big enough to fit 40 football fields' – designed as an all-weather 'one-stop destination for business and leisure', 'a synergistic combination of activities and variety available round-the-clock'. This development is just across the way from the Palace of the Golden Horses and the Mines, both already in existence. The Palace of the Golden Horses, more than five-star hotel, is undoubtedly the ultimate in postmodern theme pastiche, modelled on and built by the developer of Sun City, the gambling complex in South Africa. Its mock St Mark's Place Venetian rearing horses outside lead on to endless opulent super-tat horsehead and horseshoe design everywhere you turn. The Mines is entertainment by boat, floating along under cover on purpose-built canals to jump off at the shop or restaurant of your choice. Such places look and feel exactly like what they are: dreams of pathological designers. They have no beauty, little humanity, but speak deliberately orchestrated volumes about the concerns of the organ-grinder. The Composites Technology City is planned as 'a futuristic, hi-tech garden city'. The Mid Valley city, located in the central business district of Kuala Lumpur, is going to house 'The Mega Mall – Asia's largest retail, food, and entertainment centre'. The Super Corridor itself is going to be aligned with a host of state-of-the-art perpendicular cities such as Puncak Sri Hartamas and Lestari Perdana. The former would allow the residents to 'conduct their business from home' through such 'teleservices' as 'tele-banking, tele-entertainment, tele-working, tele-conferencing'. The latter provides 'the perfect location and comes with perfect architectural design, perfect finishes and recreational and entertainment facilities that are second to none'. Dotted across the Super Corridor are smart schools to engineer a new generation of IT-savvy Malaysians. Telemedicine would ensure that those who could not cope with technology running amok would have instant access to a 'flagship' health care system based on remote consultation, diagnosis and treatment, virtual patient records and immediate teleport to a hospital.

Even the pop-electronic fanzine *Wired* described the project as 'Xanadu for Nerds'. It is a vision that does not so much reimagine Kuala Lumpur as obliterate it totally as a recognizable entity in its own future. Malaysia might have been saved from much of this technocratic dystopia by the collapse of the Asian markets, had not Mahathir just kept on pushing, ploughing the national wealth into his overarching vision. As an attempt to create an information-age metropolis, the Super Corridor was not a bad idea, if you strip it of a goodly number of its megalomaniac components. The industrial city is rapidly becoming obsolete. A post-industrial borderless metropolis in which technology plays a central role is taking its place. But Mahathir was never interested in creating a borderless metropolis; his dream was more specific – a centralized, electronic megalopolis with well-defined boundaries. The historic trend is away from the centre of the city and to a more dispersed pattern of growth, with economic activities spreading out to what are dubbed 'edge cities' or cities *à la carte*. Here, living and working patterns of individuals and communities shape the borderless borders of the city. But in Mahathir's cyberdream it is not just the buildings that are controlled: individuals and communities are also treated as though they had no will or needs of their own. The drive to achieve the vision is as imperious as the practice of local developers who habitually give long-established squatter communities a few days' notice to leave their houses before they are bulldozed. People go on holiday and return to discover embryonic flyovers passing over their homes or a motorway being built before their front door. In the notorious, and abandoned, Bakun hydroelectrical dam project in Sarawak, over ten thousand *orang asli* homes were flooded, so that in a bizarre scheme the dam could be linked via an undersea submarine electricity cable to Kuala Lumpur.

The natural tendency of new information technology is to decentralize the city, spread it out in all directions. Mahathir has used technology to centralize and control Kuala Lumpur. More and more high-tech developments were dumped in the centre of the city, concentrating economic activities, office spaces and shopping complexes in a very small area. The end result was an apocalyptic gridlock. The Petronas Twin Towers alone had the capacity to place two million extra cars right in the centre of Kuala Lumpur. The Multimedia Super Corridor is not an accommodation to the likely shape of future needs but, in essence, a feudal dream. In practice, it will enhance the power of the Malaysian ruling class and make the rich richer. All that is required of the rest of the nation is to ogle at the magic of the marvel in its midst. Indeed, the segments of the plan already implemented had precisely this effect, encouraged by the eulogies in specially made television documentaries that stress again and again that these lavish designs are Malaysia's just deserts. Despite Mahathir's renowned anti-Western rhetoric, he envisioned and set about creating an imperial enclave overwriting Kuala Lumpur and stretching beyond. It was a new landscape, one that was only possible as a neo-imperialist outpost of global capitalism, as a ready-built, for-the-convenience-of-others invitation to the foreign investment he excoriated during the economic crisis. Visionary dreams apart, the only thing that will make the MSC work, if it ever can, is a new dependency, an abandonment of subversion and resistance in favour of servicing a world made elsewhere. It is not a dream that can be fulfilled from within Malaysia's own enterprise by home-grown initiative as it currently exists. The magical new cities that will obliterate the old Kuala Lumpur are unimaginable without the expatriates, relocated by the multinational corporations that are being wooed and coddled, persuaded and invited to set up shop in the Super Corridor. Off-centre of the resilience of Kuala Lumpur to overcome colonialism, a new pattern reinstituting the old colonial career is being made. Even the much-touted Cyber University relies on expatriate expertise. The rural poor could benefit from the mega-projects only through the vagaries of trickle-down theory which itself has all but trickled out of sensible economic thinking. Moreover, Mahathir's dreamscape relies almost totally on the old transfer of technology thesis, betting on buying innovation, rather than creating an innovative culture at home. After all, he suggested on numerous occasions,

232

if Malaysia can develop a national car – based on a Japanese original – it can make anything. The location of corporate research and development operations in Kuala Lumpur would automatically transform Malaysia into a dynamic, research-based knowledge society. The realities of the structure of international labour, the myopic and parochial interests of monopoly capital and multinational corporations, the local inability to develop and provide a lock-on to such corporate capital and technology just did not enter the picture. Nor did the inconsistencies pro-vided by the presence of open repression on the streets of Kuala Lumpur, or the even more pertinent demonstration of Mahathir's efforts to prevent the repatriation of investment and profits in order to ease the refinancing of his futuristic economic vision. Mahathir's technodreams have little to do with self-sufficiency, democracy and decency and much to do with absolute power.

The end of the 1990s dislocated both Kuala Lumpur and its denizens. The city lost its identity, its diverse and varied spaces becoming more and more submerged, monolithic and banal, its perspective evaporated in a meaninglessness riot of high-tech, late modernity. It was subjugated to, and imprisoned in, the will to power of a single man. For the vast majority of its inhabitants, Kuala Lumpur entered not a future vision but a twilight zone. The institutions of the state became enemies of the people. The ruthlessly controlled press and broadcasting became instruments of disinformation giving out the government line on the façade of sexual scandal that no one believed to be true. Mind control and how it could be escaped became the dominant game of the city. In futuristic utopias, information is equated with power; but credulity, an age-old human device, it seems, is also a rubber band capable of snapping people back to reality. Democratic free-doms serviced by the free flow of information have never been part of the idealistic vision nor the natural reflexes of Mahathir. Only one politician in Malaysia represented and, so far as he was able, practised these ideas. Only Anwar genuinely believed their practical realization had to become the lived reality of the nation. His straightforward answers on these points often left visiting

The house Mahathir built: the controversial Prime Minister's residence in the visionary new city of Putra Jaya.

journalists open-mouthed. It is a fitting testimony to the resilience of reality in the Malaysian setting that, even from prison, Anwar engendered more genuine freedom of creative activity and opened more floodgates of free information than Mahathir could ever manage. The mosque in Kampung Baru became a frequent starting point for demonstrations, from which issued crowds of young people to be viciously beaten by riot-geared police. The same spirit stirred in the mosques of other villages in the city, such as Kampung Dato Keramat. And the greatest annoyance of all in a groundswell of dissent that would not simply fade away was that the Internet, the basis of Mahathir's megalomaniacal dreams, became the locus of all the information he would not permit to circulate in real-time reality. Subversion within the forms of conformity has long been the Malay way, the resilience that has enabled Malay society to adapt and survive with its identity and traditional roots intact. In the Mahathir years a new generation of Malaysians has grown up. They have watched the fight of the elephants and seen the alternate visions of the future these contestants carried into the fight. On the streets of Kuala Lumpur the tea stalls are a natural focus of discussion of everything in a city where there are no secrets.

Mahathir sent his police agents to listen for subversive talk. He also had them try to sabotage the free flow of information on the Internet. But none of it could succeed in bottling up a genuinely new, handmade, home-grown spirit of defiance among the people of Kuala Lumpur, a gathering drawn from all of Malaysia. And, once discovered, the spirit of dissent – as I know so well, having tasted it myself – never leaves an individual, or a community, or a society. Young and old together have found they have resources outside official channels and resilience to resist the climate of authoritarian repression they never knew or dreamed they possessed. In trying to banish the light at the end of the tunnel that most Malaysians assumed, complacently, would right the all-too-obvious wrongs in their society without any effort on their part, Mahathir has succeeded in focusing their minds on the choice facing the nation. Is it to be an ordered society which is a parody of supposedly traditional Malay conformism, straitjacketed by a feudal order that turns all its citizens into dependent clients who can be easily divided, manipulated and controlled? Or should and will they create the society envisioned, already extant in cyberspace rather than built in bricks and mortar in Cyberjaya? The vision, reflected in the postings on the Internet from Malay, Chinese and Indian Malaysians, loudly proclaims their belief in the mature inheritance of a genuinely democratic multiracial Malaysia, an open society that is open to the outside world, without formal communal structures. It would be a society that has consigned feudal lords and formalized patronage to the proverbial dustbin of history. It is this option that has been embraced by the new collective opposition in Malaysia, an opposition sustained by the genuine resilience of what the Malays call *gotong-royong*, co-operation and self-help. They have discovered that their battle is for far more than the rescue of one man and dethroning of another: it is the challenge to rescue and revive the collective best ideals of an entire society. The established order has inordinate power and control at its command; the people of Malaysia have few resources to back their defiance. Their only strength is the lure of a moment

235

of choice, the chance to take decision making about their future into their own hands. But the desire for freedom has countless other unknown strengths; that is why it always finds ways to overcome the will to power.

III

Bond villains, as we all know, always get their come-uppance. *Sejarah Malayu* also suggests power has a weak underbelly and limited life. In an obscure passage, we read the story of the clever people of Alam in Sumatra. Once upon a time, they were besieged by a mighty army, complete with a herd of killer buffaloes, from Majapahit in northeast Java. There was no way they could defeat such an army. One of their leaders suggested to the Majapahit commanders that the battle be settled without bloodshed. Let us resolve the conflict with a buffalo fight, he said. If our buffalo loses, we will surrender; if your buffalo is defeated, then you must withdraw. The Majapahit commanders, arrogant in their power, proud of their buffaloes and knowing too well that the people of Alam had only tame, farming buffaloes, had no qualms. They sent a gigantic, ferocious beast to do battle. The people of Alam brought a suckling calf. It had not drunk for a week and had a necklace of poisonous thorns attached to its horns. When the two animals were set free in a designated open ground, the calf ran immediately to the big bull and started searching for its teats. Its horns scratched the skin of the buffalo; and the poisonous thorns performed their magic. In a few minutes, the poisoned buffalo fell to the ground. The Majapahit army withdrew. Ever since, the people of Alam have been known as *minang-karbau*, victorious buffalo!

The old bull appears to be invincible. But the creative spirit of the sucking calves of democracy will not subside. The next rebuilding of Kuala Lumpur is being forged in battle.

Select Bibliography

Abdullah, Firdaus Haji, *Radical Malay Politics: Its Origins and Early Development* (Kuala Lumpur, 1985)

Anwar, Zainah, *Islamic Revivalism in Malaysia* (Kuala Lumpur, 1987)

Bird, Isabella, *The Golden Chersonese: Travels in Malaya in 1879* (Singapore, 1967)

Gale, Bruce, *Readings in Malaysian Politics* (Kuala Lumpur, 1986)

Gullick, J. M., *The Story of Kuala Lumpur, 1857–1939* (Petaling Jaya, 1983)

——, *Kuala Lumpur, 1880–1895: A City in the Making* (Kuala Lumpur, 1988)

——, *Old Kuala Lumpur* (Kuala Lumpur, 1994)

Ibrahim, Anwar, *The Asian Renaissance* (Kuala Lumpur, 1996)

Khoo Boo Teik, *Paradoxes of Mahathirism* (Kuala Lumpur, 1995)

Khoo Kay Kim, *Kuala Lumpur: The Formative Years* (Kuala Lumpur, 1996)

Maaruf, Shaharuddin, *Concept of a Hero in Malay Society* (Singapore, 1984)

——, *Malay Ideas on Development: From Feudal Lord to Capitalist* (Singapore, 1988)

Mohamad, Mahathir, *The Malay Dilemma* (Kuala Lumpur, 1970)

Morais, Victor, *Anwar Ibrahim* (Kuala Lumpur, 1983)

Muzaffar, Chandra, *Freedom in Fetters: An Analysis of the State of Democracy in Malaysia* (Penang, 1986)

Omar, Asmah Haji, *Language and Society in Malaysia* (Kuala Lumpur, 1982)

——, *Malay in its Sociocultural Context* (Kuala Lumpur, 1987)

Osman, Mohd Taib, *Bunga Rampai: Aspects of Malay Culture* (Kuala Lumpur, 1984)

Spruit, Ruud, *The Land of the Sultans* (Amsterdam, 1995)

Sweeney, Amin, *Malay Word Music: A Celebration of Oral Creativity* (Kuala Lumpur, 1994)

Talib, Rokiah, and Tan, Chee-Beng, eds, *Dimensions of Tradition and Development in Malaysia* (Kuala Lumpur, 1995)

Vlatseas, S., *The Wizard of KL* (Petaling Jaya, 1977)

Winstedt, Richard, *A History of Classical Malay Literature* (Kuala Lumpur, 1960)

——, *The Malay Magician* (Singapore, 1961)

——, *Malay Proverbs* (Singapore, 1981)

Photographic Acknowledgements

The authors and publishers wish to express their thanks to the following sources of illustrative material and/or permission to reproduce it:

John Apicella/Cesar Pelli & Associates: p. 39; Barnaby's Picture Library: pp. 34, 35, 38, 40, 68, 80, 93, 101, 117, 131, 189; by permission of the Syndics of Cambridge University Library: pp. 47, 48, 62–3, 92, 114; Gerald Cubitt: pp. 40, 131; courtesy of John Falconer: pp. 59, 61, 65; from the freemalaysia home page [http://www.freemalaysia.com]: p. 234; Keith N. Radford: pp. 34, 68, 80, 93, 101, 117.